History of the Illinois Conference United Church of Christ

JACK FAY ROBINSON

EXPLORATION PRESS
Chicago, Illinois

Printed in the United States of America

Exploration Press
Chicago Theological Seminary
5757 University Avenue
Chicago, Illinois 60637

CTS ISBN NO.: 0-913552-43-7

Library of Congress Catalog Card Number: 90-081374

Contents

Preface

One of the little known treasures located at The Chicago Theological Seminary has been the Exploration Press. Its capacity to publish several scholarly works over the years has been primarily dependent upon the hard work of two of the Seminary's senior faculty members, Dr. Perry LeFevre, Professor of Constructive Theology and Dr. W. Widick Schroeder, Professor of Religion and Society.

Exploration Press is operated independently of the Seminary with the "love and caring" of these two faculty members. It has provided an opportunity for a select groups of theological scholars to contribute to our on-going theological dialogue in the theological seminary community, in the churches and in other circles.

This is the first time that the Press has published a more popular work. It has done so in the interest of the Illinois Conference of the United Church of Christ, the churches and people of the churches and for those students interested in a detailed account of the events and persons which have shaped the Illinois Conference.

We must always take care to retrieve our histories, our personal and family histories. History provides us with some clues of why we are what we are today. Institutional histories are extremely important. Institutions do have impact upon society for better or worse. They are shaped by events and people who have visions, ideas, and mission. In order to have more influence, people join others in forming institutions and voluntary associations.

In a volume honoring the work of James Luther Adams on voluntary associations, edited by J. Ronald Engel, there is a chapter in which Adams writes on the Voluntary Principle in the Forming of American Religion.

> "Many people entertain attitudes in favor of freedom, but socially effective freedom requires participation in associations that define or redefine freedom and

that attempt to articulate or implement that freedom in a specific social milieu." (p. 173)

The Illinois Conference of the United Church of Christ is an example of the kind of voluntary association about which Adams wrote. United Church of Christ churches, with the support of the individual members of those churches, covenanted to create the Conference. Its mission was and continues to be to bear witness to the living Christ in that part of Illinois it serves.

The pages which follow contain the story of events and people which created and sustained the Conference through the years. They tell the stories of faithful people, their churches and related institutions which in concert have been the Illinois Conference family.

We are indebted to the Rev. Jack Fay Robinson for this book which helps to remember from whence the Conference came. We are grateful to the Rev. Dr. W. Sterling Cary, Conference Minister, and the entire staff of Illinois Conference of the United Church of Christ for the assistance they gave in making possible Mr. Robinson's work.

Kenneth B. Smith, President
The Chicago Theological Seminary

From Four Lanes to One

Four traditions of American Protestantism were united in Illinois when an Acting Conference of the United Church of Christ was established in 1963. Three of these strands had made important contributions to the area most of the time since Illinois became a state in 1918. The fourth, the Reformed Church, had been represented by less than a handful of churches. It was shortly after the War of 1812 that the first Congregational ministers began work in the Illinois area. By 1833 at least five Congregational churches had been formed in the state. The seeds of the German Evangelical Synod of North America were planted in 1840, largely in the St. Louis area; however, one of the founders was from Quincy. The first Evangelical Church in Chicago was founded in 1843.

Early church work was greatly influenced by the regions from which the settlers came. Many had migrated from the New England states, an early stronghold of Congregationalism. Most of the early pastors came from that section of the country.

During the years from 1812 to 1882 more than a quarter of a million people migrated from Germany, many of them settling in Illinois. The motive for this migration has been stated simply by Dr. Rudolf G. Schade: "The reasons for the great migration must be seen in the economic opportunities offered to the various craftsmen, the possibility to acquire land, the attempt to escape military service, to live in a land in which the dream of a democratic political system had become a historic reality. The beauty of the land and the economic opportunities had been much publicized in German magazines and journals."

During the early part of the nineteenth century, the Congregationalists and the Presbyterians combined their efforts under a Plan of Union. Believing that the Presbyterian type of organization was better suited to the frontier, even Congregational ministers organized churches in that manner. However, by 1840 this cooperation had largely run its course. The causes for this change were brought about by differences in church polity, theology, and above all, the question of slavery. Rev. H.L. Hammond, pastor of the Hampshire Colony Congregational Church in Princeton, claimed to send the first petition to free the slaves to Abraham Lincoln in 1861. Although there is no supporting evidence for that claim, there is no question concerning the petition delivered to the President the following year from a group meeting in the First Congregational Church of Chicago.

Most of the early churches were organized in central and southern Illinois. The first Congregational Association was founded in 1835 by churches in Quincy, Jacksonville and others in that general region. Similar groups were organized as the Fox River Association (1835), and Rock River in 1838. The Chicago Congregational Association was not formed until 1853.

The Christian Church, with independent roots in Virginia, North Carolina, Vermont and Pennsylvania, also began its work during the early years of Illinois history. One of the first Christian preachers was William Kincaid, who settled in Lawrence County about 1817, and was a member of the Illinois Constitutional Convention, and was important in keeping slavery out of the state. The oldest Christian church still in existence was founded in 1839 — Bethlehem church in Lukin township, near Sumner. The southern Illinois Christian Conference made its appearance in 1833. Other early conferences include Spoon River (1838), Central Illinois (1852), Fox River (1856), Western Illinois (1857), Major River and Jacksonville (1861). In 1883 the Illinois State Christian Conference was formed. The history of these churches is little known because there are few records. Dr. Matthew Spinka explained this: "We are informed that the early fathers, fearing the dead hand of the past might hold sway over them, were in the habit of burning the minutes of the meetings soon after they were held!"

The membership of the Christian churches in Illinois dropped from its highest, 8,000 members in 1910, to only 5,620 in 1931. It is not surprising that discussions to disband the Illinois State Conference began as early as 1918. These discussions were held in Merom, Indiana, the site of a college dating back to 1860, and still the site of meetings for churches in that region. The possibility of merger with the Congregational churches was discussed in 1913, and approved by the General Convention of the Christian church in 1926. The following year similar action was taken by the Congregational churches meeting in Omaha. The Christian churches of Illinois met in LaGrange in 1931 and unanimously adopted a resolution to unite with the Congregational churches. The Congregational Conference of Illinois, meeting in the same city, duplicated the Christian churches action to merge. So it was that two traditions of the future United Church of Christ were combined.

It should be stated that this merger between two hitherto separate denominations did create some problems. Rev. Carl D. Hall, the last minister to be ordained by the Christian church before its first merger, writes: "In the early years of the Congregational and Christian merger many discussions were held and some became rather heated, many members thinking they would betray their ancestors by voting for the merger. At one of the early State Conferences I attended in the early years of the Congregational Christian Conference, the Congregational members sat on one side of the church and the Christians on the opposite side. Gradually as we came to know each other better, these differences disappeared and it helped lay the groundwork for the union 25 years ago with the Evangelical and Reformed churches, for both denominations believed as one of their principles in 'The union of all followers of Christ.'"

The work of the Evangelical Church in this part of the country was first centered in the St. Louis area and in southern Illinois. One early missionary was located in Alton in 1832. However, when Chicago was a small town of about 4,000, St. Paul's church was founded in the city by the Evangelicals in 1843. This church was the site of the meeting which organized the denomination later known as the Missouri Synod Lutheran, a group of which St. Paul's was never a member. It was also at St. Paul's in 1877 that action was taken to form the German Evangelical Synod of North America. The pastor of the same church was instrumental in the founding of what later became known as Elmhurst College.

Another group of German immigrants to the United States had formed the Reformed Church in the United States. These people had largely settled in Pennsylvania. Talks of merger with the Evangelical Church had begun in 1927. In June 1934 the two denominations met in Cleveland, Ohio, and formed the Evangelical and Reformed Church. Thus, the second merger of traditions which later became the Illinois Conference of the United Church of Christ were brought together. There were only a few congregations from this Reformed group in the Illinois area. The North Illinois Synod of the Evangelical and Reformed Church was organized in 1938. Rev. Dr. William Rest, who became the first Minister of the United Church of Christ Conference in Illinois, held the position of President of the North Illinois Synod from 1941, the last eight years in a full-time capacity.

As times changed so did the work and emphases of the churches. The Congregational churches moved from anti-slavery to women's organizations to conservative Puritan teachings, to pacifism, and so on. The first women's organization formed in a local church was in First Church, Rockford in 1838, the start of a movement which superceded the slavery issue. One cause of the change was the fact that membership changed from rural to heavily urban. The Women's Board of Missions in the Interior was organized in 1868. Their missionary work expanded to include work among the American Indians.

The magazine, *Congregational Herald* made its appearance in Chicago in 1854. The denominational magazine, *The Advance*, began publication in Chicago in 1867. The work of church members in Illinois extended far beyond the boundaries of the state. The chief author of the "Kansas City Creed," a religious statement adopted by Congregationalists in 1913, was Rev. William Barton, pastor of the First Congregational Church of Oak Park. The first General Secretary of Congregational Brotherhoods, established in 1918, was Rev. Frank Dyer, pastor of the Waveland Avenue church in Chicago.

The church was naturally affected by wider economic conditions. Due to the depressed economy, in 1936 the position of Superintendent of the Illinois

Conference was abolished and three areas were established: Chicago, Northern and Southern. The Northern area was headed by Rev. Nels Nordstrom, the Southern by Rev. Walter Schlaretzki, and the Chicago area was taken over by the General Director of the Chicago Congregational Union, Rev. Neil Hanson. This arrangement remained until May 4, 1954, when the Rev. Frank L. Edwards was installed as Superintendent of the CC Conference. He was succeeded by Rev. Clarence McCall in 1959, and by Rev. James R. Smucker in 1963. He served as executive of the Acting Conference until the merger was completed the following year. As a footnote, it might be added that it took time for the Congregatonalists to be unified. It was stated by a superintendent from another conference, that the three area directors never sat together at their meetings!

Closely related to the Illinois Conference has been the organization now known as the Community Renewal Society (CRS), but which has operated under various names over the years. It was organized in 1882 as the Chicago City Missionary Society by Congregational ministers and lay people to serve the needs of the city. Originally concerned with the needs of recent immigrants, it has continued this approach down through the years. The needs of Black people from the south became apparent. In 1911 the first Black graduate of the Chicago Theological Seminary began work by founding Lincoln Memorial Church which was admitted to the Chicago Congregational Association in 1919. Its building was made possible by the Society. In more recent years the religious needs of the growing Hispanic population have been met in large part by the Union's successor, CRS. It was the executive of this organization who took over guiding the work of Congregational churches in the Chicago area following the Great Depression. Although an independent organization, it has usually been closely related to the Congregational Churches, then the Congregational Christian churches, and now, the United Church of Christ, in the metropolitan area.

The various institutions founded by the predecessors of the United Church of Christ have made, and still make, a very significant contribution to the life of the Illinois Conference. One important contribution has been in the field of education. Illinois College for Men was founded in 1829. Knox College followed seven years later. Rockford College for Women opened its doors soon after, followed by Beloit College in Wisconsin. Merom Institute began its work in Indiana in 1862.

The educational work of the Evangelical Church included parochial schools during the early years. Religious training was provided in higher education as well. A theological seminary was opened in Marysville, Missouri, in 1850. It became Eden Seminary in 1883. Although not located in Illinois, Eden has been the seminary for training many of the pastors throughout the Conference. Another school was opened in Lake Zurich in 1868. It was transferred to Elmhurst in 1871, and gained distinction in the succeeding years as Elmhurst College.

Many of the early Congregational ministers were trained at Yale and Andover (now Andover Newton). Early Evangelical ministers received additional training at Hartford en route to the frontier. The Chicago Theological Seminary began its mission in 1855, the oldest institute of higher learning in Chicago. From modest beginnings, it soon expanded. In 1882 it introduced a German department. Never an "Ivory Tower" as its former president Arthur Cushman McGiffert Jr. stated in his history of the seminary, CTS has had a distinguished record for training ministers for the ever-changing needs and opportunities of the Conference territory, and regions far beyond. This seminary, as well as the Community Renewal Society and the Chicago YMCA, received substantial aid from the estate of Victor Lawson, noted newspaper publisher and Congregational layman, in 1925.

Several other institutions closely related to the churches are a vital part of the history, background and accomplishments of the Illinois Conference of the United Church of Christ. It was in 1893 that thirteen pastors of the German Evangelical Synod met in Palatine and laid the foundation for which is now The Bensenville Home Society. It was the following year when the German Evangelical Orphanage and the Old Peoples' Home Society of Northern Illinois actually were organized at a meeting in St. Peter's Church, Chicago. Uhlich Children's Home in Chicago also has been a mission of the churches.

The needs of the elderly became a growing concern during the first half of the twentieth century. This concern, first expressed in the founding of the Bensenville Home, was expanded by the establishment of St. Paul's Home for the Elderly in Chicago in 1922. In 1937 the Congregationalists began conversations which led to the founding of Plymouth Place in LaGrange Park in 1944. Peace Memorial Home in Evergreen Park and the Good Samaritan Home of Quincy have also been agencies closely associated with the people of the conference.

Hospital care has always been a form of ministry. The work of the Evangelical Health Systems dates back to 1906. It includes Christ Hospital in Oak Lawn, Good Samaritan Hospital in Downers Grove, Good Shepherd Hospital in Barrington, Bethany Hospital in Chicago. South Chicago Hospital has recently been added. Each one has various facilities located in the northeast section of the state. The many-sided ministry carried on by these agencies are a vital part of the story of the United Church Conference of Illinois. They are, however, independent one of another. Each is entitled to longer treatment, not possible in a brief survey of the Conference.

The movement for Christian unity made great strides on the national level in the formation of the United Church of Christ in 1957. The merger of regional, state and metropolitan work soon followed. So it was that the North Illinois Synod of the Evangelical and Reformed Church and the Congregational Christian Conference of Illinois became Acting Conference of the UCC in 1963.

Transition 1960-1964

According to hearsay, the United Church of Christ movement started with a ministers' meeting in the St. Louis area in the 1940s. It is said that conversations between ministers and the Evangelical and Reformed Church and of the Congregational Christian churches led them to the conclusion that they really had so much in common that denominational differences, great as they were, were secondary to their common faith, and they should unite. This conviction was in keeping with the cooperation of many denominations as well as the denominational unions and mergers which were gaining a foothold increasingly as the twentieth century advanced.

It takes time and effort, however, as well as conviction, to achieve such a goal. On the national level the United Church of Christ was organized in 1957. On the conference and synodical levels it required much more time. The support of local churches must be achieved. Great differences in worship, theology and church polity had to be bridged. So it was that a period of preparation and transition was in order. After several years of discussion, meetings and voting, the North Illinois Synod of the Evangelical and Reformed Church and the Illinois Conference of Congregational Christian Churches became Acting Conferences of the newly organized United Church of Christ in 1963. The actual union of the Conference was not consummated until the following year.

The problems to be solved were varied and complex. One denomination was organized on the Presbyterian model, the other, Congregational. One group had a statement of faith, the other expressed its beliefs in terms of a creed and catechism. The worship of one was liturgical, while the other varied widely in its worship services. These were all differences which had led to divisions in the church for centuries. One striking illustration of differences can be seen in the name of one of the committees in the North Illinois Synod: Committee on Registration and Excuses. The implication that excuses are required for non-attendance at meetings was totally foreign to the other group.

There were other problems, too, not religious in nature, but sociological. The congregations were located in vastly different settings. Some were closely connected with large metropolitan areas. Since the Illinois area had two such regions, those connected socially and economically with Chicago and St. Louis, that problem was ultimately settled by the formation of two UCC conferences.

A large segment of Illinois, however, is either rural or small town. This is not a "religious" difference, but it has led to differences among the churches. One of the tasks of Rev. Kurt Schmiechen, a member of the first Conference board, was to interpret the attitudes and ways of small congregations to those whose experience had been with larger ones. There has always been somewhat of a gulf between Chicago and downstate Illinois. With these differences and others to overcome, it is little wonder that several years were required before the dream of a United Church of Christ Illinois Conference could become a reality. The creation of the Illinois South Conference was probably inevitable.

An early step toward union was taken in the formation of a Joint Study and Advisory Committee, June 22, 1960, by the Congregational Christian group, and included only its own members. The following individuals were appointed:

Rev. C.F. McCall Jr.	Rev. James R. Smucker
Thomas Hook	Harry E. Kellogg
Mrs. Arthur McLaughlin	John E Livingston Jr.
Rev. Edward F. Manthei	Rev. Vernon E. Loescher
Mrs. Robert Reneker	Mrs. Lester Mitchell
	Stewart P. Mulvihill
	Robert H. White

The individuals in the second column were reappointed May 4, 1961, and again May 10, 1962.

The Board of Trustees of the Congregational Christian Conference moved out ahead by passing a resolution March 15, 1961. After voting to recommend to the forthcoming meeting of the Conference that it become an Acting Conference of the United Church of Christ, it stated:

> Be it further resolved that the Congregational and Christian Conference of Illinois, when acting as a Conference of the United Church of Christ, proceed with utmost dispatch to confer with synods of the Evangelical and Reformed Church and other groups acting as conferences of the United Church of Christ concerning the reorganization of a conference of the United Church of Christ on a territorial basis.

The churches, however, had other ideas. When the North Illinois Synod of the Evangelical and Reformed Church met on April 25, 1961, Rev. William L. Rest recommended that no vote be taken at that time. It seems that less than one-third of the Congregational Christian churches in Illinois had voted for the merger. There was no desire to unite with a small minority of the other denomination. It was also voted by the Synod that there should be one, not two or three, conference in the state. It was further recommended that each of the following synods have one representative on the Joint Study and Advisory Committee: Midwest Synod, South Indiana Synod, German Conference and the Magyar Synod.

The North Illinois Synod voted to become an Acting Conference of the United Church of Christ on April 21, 1961, at a meeting in St. John's Church, Freeport. The vote in favor of the proposed constitution was:

In favor	212
Opposed	39

The first really *Joint* Study and Advisory Committee by both groups had representatives of the three ecclesiastical bodies which were seriously considering the organization of one Illinois Conference. The members selected were:

South Illinois Synod -
Rev. G.A. Friz
William Hendrich
Rev Paul Schlauter
Rev. Paul Surbey, Secy.
Rev. Robert Tormohlen
Joseph Wetzel
Dr. John L. Schmidt, ex officio

North Illinois Synod -
Rev. Walter Klaffmann
Francis Mies
Paul Nebold
Norman Reuss
Rev. Paul Umbeck
Dr. William L. Rest, ex officio

Congregational Christian Conference -
Rev. Charles C. Hoskinson, Chair
Harry E. Kellogg
John H. Livengood Jr.
Rev. Vernon A. Loescher
Mrs. Lester Mitchell
Stewart P. Mulvihill
Rev. Oliver Powell
Rev. Lester Smith
Rev. James R. Smucker
Robert H. White
Rev. Clarence McCall, ex officio

The proposed constitution of the Illinois Conference was acted on by the Congregational Christian Conference of Illinois at the annual meeting at the First Congregational Church, Moline, May 7-9, 1963. Rev. Charles C. Hoskinson introduced the resolution to adopt the proposed constitution. It was believed that the South Illinois Synod would become a part of the new organization. A preliminary approval of that body had indicated acceptance, a decision reversed soon after.

The Congregational Christian Conference devoted a good deal of the meeting to discussion of the document. The question was raised concerning the effectiveness of the large Associations proposed, but received no support at that time. Parenthetically, it might be noted that the formation of Mission Councils in 1972 provided for smaller units within each of the Associations. The meeting voted "in principle" for the proposed constitution. Rev. James R. Smucker reported to the North Illinois Synod that the vote was:

Yes 400	No 1	Abstention 1

The state was set for the formation of the new Conference.

The Constituting Conference of the Illinois Conference of the United Church of Christ was held at First Congregational Church, Oak Park, February 4-5, 1964. In keeping with the precedent started by the national organization, major positions were filled by one individual from each of the uniting bodies.

Co-Moderators:	Rev. M.J.A. Dalrymple	- CC
	Rev. Kurt Schmiechen	- E&R
Co-Scribes:	Mrs. A.M. Hainer	- CC
	Rev. Dean Plassmann	- E&R

The proposed constitution was presented by Rev. Charles C. Hoskinson.

The changes adopted were largely due to the fact that the South Illinois Synod had voted not to become a part of the Illinois Conference. References which included in any way the South Illinois Synod were changed. In addition the Southwest Division was not organized. Changes in some of the titles were made, such a Chairman and Vice Chairman to President and Vice President of the Board of Directors. The changes recommended by the Joint Study and Advisory Council were adopted. Most of those presented from the floor lost.

Separate meetings were held by the two bodies. The delegates and ministers of the North Illinois Synod recessed to the First Baptist Church for their special meeting. The Congregational Christian lay delegates and ministers recessed to the sanctuary of the First Congregational Church. Both groups voted unanimous approval. The minutes record the formal decision:

> The co-moderators declared the documents approved and called upon the Rev. Joseph Evans, the Rev. William L. Rest, the Rev. James R. Smucker, and the Rev. Dean G. Plassman to affix the signatures and seal of office to the document of the Articles of Agreement for consolidation. The documents were signed and witnessed to by the delegates of the conference.

The assembly arose, and as an expression of praise and thanksgiving sang the Doxology. The Rev. Fred Hoskins, former co-president of the United Church of Christ and former pastor in the conference, offered the Prayer of Consolidation.

It was then moved by Rev. James R. Smucker that fifteen commissions be established. Nine of these commissions should consist of eleven members, two from each association, and three elected at large. The Christian Education Commission should consist of one representative of each association for each of its four sub-committees, and four elected at large. The Commission on Lay Life and Work should have three representatives from each association (one layman, one laywoman, one minister), plus six representatives elected at large, and representation from the other commissions in the Division of Parish Life.

The commissioners of the Conference were to be grouped under four divisions: (1) Administration, (2) Church and Ministry, (3) Church and Society, and (4) Parish Life. Provision was also made for the selection of the staff of the newly formed Conference. There were some, who regarded themselves as naive on looking back through the years, who felt the political maneuvering and behind-the-scene strategies for positions were scandalous in the Church. A resolution was passed recommending a covenant with the Chicago City Missionary Society whereby it would share responsibility for inner-city ministry and urban planning in the Chicago metropolitan area with the Conference. The Director of the Society would become a member of the Conference Staff.

Russell Palmer, chair of the Registration Committee, reported attendance at the Constituting Conference:

	E&R	**C C**	**Total**
Churches	114	175	289
Ministers	148	176	324
Delegates	114	207	321
Visitors	8	50	58
	270	433	703

The Conference closed with the service of Communion. The officiating ministers were Rev. M.J.A. Dalrymple, Rev. Kurt Schmeichen, Rev. William Rest, Rev. James Smucker and Rev. Oliver Powell. The conference meditation was given by Rev. Gerhard Grauer, moderator of the General Synod of the United Church of Christ.

The first annual meeting of the Illinois Conference was held at Illinois State University, Normal, June 9-11, 1965. There were 608 registrations reported as follows:

	CC	**E & R**	**Total UCC**
Churches	138	121	259
Ministers	162	135	297
Lay Delegates	131	90	221
Visitors	69	21	90
Total UCC			608

The necessary legal steps were taken and officers and staff duly elected. The matter of location of the Conference Headquarters took time to settle. Rev.

Kenneth Smith, chairperson of the Headquarters Committee, reported on the various locations which had been considered. This complex issue was finally settled in favor of a location in Hinsdale, in the building which had housed St. John's Church.

The Personnel Committee, chaired by Rev. Oliver Powell, placed in nomination Rev. William L. Rest as Conference Minister. Representatives of the Associations placed in nomination the following nominations for Association Ministers: Rev. James R. Smucker, Northeast; Rev. Louis H. Lammert, Central; Rev. Donald R. Scott, Southern. All the foregoing nominees were elected. The Northern Association made its nomination later: The following officers were then elected:

President: Rev. Joseph H. Evans
Vice President: Rev. John F. Schmidt
Secretary: Mrs. R.K. Wobbe
Treasurer: Henry E. Kellogg

Members of the Conference Board of Directors, fifteen Commissions, the nominating committee, and delegates to the General Synod were duly elected. The budget was adopted. Resolutions were passed on the following subjects: Health Insurance, Conference Newspaper, Orderly Transition of program, Southern Association (located outside the territory), Vacancies on Commissions and Committees, Racial Justice Now, Open Housing, Desegregated Education, Public Aid, and others. The concluding official act was the election of Mr. Walter S. Grotefelt (member of Bethany Church, Chicago) as moderator, and Rev. Donald S. Bourne (minister of Federated Church, Sycamore) as vice moderator. The organization of the Illinois Conference of the United Church of Christ was now completed. The task of carrying on its work was to begin.

Getting Started: THE ADMINISTRATION OF WILLIAM L. REST 1964-1968

The first annual meeting of the newly formed Illinois Conference of the United Church of Christ merely set the stage for the opening act. There were staff members to be selected, and many details to be carried out. This situation was clearly stated by Rev. Rest whose address to the Conference June 14, 1966, was reported in the year book.

> "He stated that as a Conference we had successfully passed the stage of consolidating two separate traditions and practices and had become one body. He felt that now we must find a way of reconciling the three historic approaches of the Church ..."

Many detailed decisions and actions were required before the Conference could launch out on its ministry.

I

The Reverend William L. Rest brought a wealth of experience to the newly created position of Conference Minister. During the previous year he had served in that capacity for the North Illinois Acting Conference. Since 1955 he had been the first full time President of the North Illinois Synod of the Evangelical and Reformed Church, the youngest person ever elected as President. William Rest had served pastorates in Indiana and Iowa before coming to churches in Elgin and Chicago. His wider experience had included being Superintendent of the Evangelical Hospital in Kansas City, Missouri, and service on the Commission on World Service of the Evangelical and Reformed Church, the Commission on Christian Unity, and board member of the Church Federation of Greater Chicago, the Bensenville Home Society, and the Council for Health and Welfare of the United Church of Christ.

II

There was a wide variety of actions to be taken before the work of the Conference could begin in any significant way. These included legal matters relating to investments, banks and real estate. In addition, it required time to build a team, not only among the staff members, but also among the four hundred churches and their 150,000 or so members. The early meetings of the Board of Directors were largely concerned with legal matters. These were related to finance and real estate. Clearly, the newly-formed not-for-profit organizations needed to arrange for the orderly transfer of these responsibilities.

There were staff members to be selected. Chosen as the Northern Association minister and associate minister of the Conference, was Rev. James Stinehelfer. Rev. James Smucker remained as minister of the Northeast Association, but Rev. Harold Dobstaff was chosen as the assistant minister. Dr. Henry Tani, director of Christian Education, served briefly until an untimely death early in 1965.

The staff members in this early period included Henry E. Kellogg, treasurer; Russell E. Palmer, assistant treasurer and business manager; Opal Moore, assistant secretary and office manager; Rev. C. Theodore Roos, director of Lay Life and Work; Rev. Donald L. Benedict, director for Urban Mission; Rev. Dean G. Plassmann, scribe, and Lois Wenzlaff and Roberta Hainer, assistant scribes. It was the task of these individuals to carry out the beginning work of the new Conference in cooperation with the churches, pastors and lay people. This was no small assignment. Since so many people were involved, the first task lay in that area.

III

In September 1964, the first issue of the Conference news was issued. This, too, was a merger. The North Illinois Synod had published *Expanding Horizons*. The Congregational Christian Conference had issued a similar paper entitled the *Illinois Conference News*. The new source of information combined the two not only in purpose, but also in name: *THE EXPANDING HORIZONS' THE ILLINOIS CONFERENCE NEWS: UNITED CHURCH OF CHRIST*. This publication was sent to all the churches during these years.

The Annual Meeting of the Conference in June 1965 was presented with a proposal for its next four years of service. Dr. Rest read his proposal dealing with program emphasis for the new Conference for the years 1965-1969. He stated: "A four year proposal is about as far into the future as our Conference should project the planning at this time."

IV

The emphasis of the United Church of Christ was called "A Thrust Toward Servanthood." Rest related the numerous studies that had been made to the task of the Church in Illinois. "Just as the search for significance has investigated three years, I would like to challenge every congregation, every Association Committee and every Conference Commission, to ask itself these basic questions.

1. How does the nature of the Church give significance to our group?
2. What obligations of Mission does this impose on us?
3. What Methods should we use to fulfill our Mission?"

It was requested that these questions be studied in terms of spirituality, outreach, service in our community, social action, stewardship and fellowship. In other words, the Thrust Toward Servanthood was a complete reevaluation of the practices and ways of the Church. The Stewardship Council of the United Church of Christ proposed that every church be visited in the fall of 1965; in fact, the Stewardship Council of the Illinois Conference already had planned that every church be visited, and each Association was making necessary preparation. This visitation was scheduled to begin September 19. Association and Conference committees were asked to make specific proposals in terms of objectives for servanthood by March 1966.

A survey of Conference giving for 1964 showed that the church members gave a little more than 2% of their income for all church purposes. Rest's proposal continues:

> If the churches plan for a real significant advance in their servanthood, an increase to 3% would be a 50% increase for both church and Conference purposes. This we believe is in the realm of possibility and should be attempted in 1966. To do this we need the most thoroughgoing preparations for a Conference-wide every member canvass. Such a preparation would require professional help and direction.

The cost of such professional help would be less than 1/2 of 1% of one year's additional income, if the goals were achieved. Dr. Rest concluded his presentation with the hope that the cost of the program would be a minor consideration.

How did these hopes and plans for the Conference work out in actual practice? The first stages were discussed in the various reports at the Fourth Annual Meeting of the Conference in June 1967. The picture is a mixed one, some successes, but hardly sufficient reason for exuberant joy. The annual report of the Board of Directors signed by John Schmidt and William L. Rest stated: "We have both pleasant and unpleasant results." The first year emphasis on The Nature and Mission of the Church resulted in better understanding of the mission in local churches on the part of many. Stewardship was the second year emphasis, and although several churches reported outstanding results, the tangible results on the whole were disappointing.

Several reasons for the relative failure of the first two years of the program were cited in the Board of Directors' report. Many of the churches were under no particular financial strain themselves, which led to the misjudgment of the readiness of the Conference churches to engage in such a program. A second reason for the disappointing results was due to the professional firm's belief that many of the things which were to be done locally were done when they were not, and the fact that the conference leadership "followed too closely the advice of the 'professionals'." Those churches which devoted a major portion of their time and effort to the program were most successful and enthusiastic.

The report continues with the information that for two successive years cutbacks in the Conference budget had been required. Not only had cuts been made in the operating budget as in the previous years, but the support of the program in urban mission, church extension and campus ministry had been reduced. The staff members had been willing to forego promised raises as well. The stewardship message was "We need more money," but rather, according to one staff member, it should have been in more positive terms, "Here are our responsibilities as Christians."

The statistics for 1966 showed a net loss of 1,427 members and eleven churches. Of the eleven churches, five were transferred to the Illinois South Conference, one consolidated with a church of another denomination. One church disbanded, and three voted out of the United Church of Christ. The churches which remained in the Conference did have an increase of 104 members. There was a slight gain in financial giving.

V

The Central Association conducted workshops on Worship in Creative Arts, Making Church Meetings Matter, and assigned advisors to small churches which were without a full-time minister. Arrangements were made for missionary speakers throughout the Association. Special concern was expressed: "How do we help our churches to go beyond being simply an institution, to becoming an instrument, from self-serving to world-serving, from being a social club to becoming truly the body of Christ, from a building or organization to an avenue." This report was submitted by Moderator Milo Phillipi and Association Minister Louis Lammert.

The Northeast Association began operating under a new structure in September 1966. There were three major boards: The Executive Council, Board of Services and the Board of Ecumenical Mission. Each did its work through a number of committees. The Board of Ecumenical Mission was also the Board of the City Missionary Society. The report, signed by Chairman of the Council Frederick Traut, and Executive Director James R. Smucker, concludes: "Although this report, of necessity, emphasizes structure and organization, we believe the efforts this year to structure for mission have already enabled us to respond more readily and effectively to the needs of the churches and the needs of the metropolitan area and the world."

The Northern Association report, submitted by Rev. William S. Mellish, moderator, and Rev. James D. Stinehelfer, minister, called the past year "the year of the great search." The relationship of the churches to one another, and of the Association to the Conference, were objects of attention. The committees, Planning and Development, Church and Ministry, and Stewardship and Christian World Mission, were engaged in laying foundations for the future. The results were stated:

> "We believe that we achieved greater unity among our Churches, that we have helped to strengthen their witness for Christ, that we have helped to increase their understanding and participation in our total denomination program and that we have challenged many of them to discover their own particular ministry."

The Wabash Association, whose name was about to be changed from Southeast, reported two meetings during the year, one being a two-day meeting around the theme, "Thy Kingdom Come." The fall meeting centered around the theme, "Call to be Servants," and was based on a questionnaire which brought mixed reactions, embarrassment, confusion and disturbance. These churches seemed to lack some understanding of the "Thrust." They did look forward with a great deal of anticipation to the forthcoming study of "The Task of Christian Education in the Small Churches," sponsored by the Conference Christian Education Committee.

VI

The Commission on Church Extension and Planning worked on several programs in response to the needs and opportunities confronting small churches, both in town and country and in urban settings. The Illinois Council and the Church Federation of Greater Chicago provided channels for much of this work. The merging of small churches, both within the Conference and across denominational lines, was a major pioneering effort of this period. Lessons learned in Chicago were helpful in providing clues for new ministries in Peoria, Moline-Rock Island, Joliet, Quincy and Danville.

The reports for the fourth Annual Meeting show the various matters which were under consideration. These included: ministerial discipline and ethics, health and welfare, theological education, social action, lay life and work, and campus ministry. The Thrust Toward Servanthood was being studied in ways to include the varied mission and opportunities which were before the new Conference.

VII

There were other problems not too clearly recognized by all the members of the Conference. One concerned the quite divergent personalities and responses of the leaders from the two branches of the newly formed Conference. To some, one group was "struck by the seeming formality ... at some gatherings. Both dress and countenance, to me at that time were stodgy." The same person added: "I was soon to learn that was not the case." From the other group there were undoubtedly those who regarded the first as not sufficiently pious and somber. It took time to overcome and outgrow such differences as these, which were every bit as important as those of worship and theology.

A second problem might be called geographical. There were large areas of rural and small town life, several large cities, and the inescapable effect of one of the nation's largest metropolitan centers. Partially related were the problems concerning proper recognition of small churches by some of those in the large congregations. This was brought to the attention of the Board during the interim period in 1969.

A third problem area in the '60s lay in the realm of social action. The services of Rev. C. Theodore Roos were loaned to the interdenominational urban ministry known as Kirchentag. Some churches were deeply involved in these questions which were foremost in the land. Other churches were bitterly opposed to social programs. This, too, was brought to the attention of the Board. Projects carried on in cooperation with the Community Renewal Society led, it was claimed, to a reduction in financial support on the part of many congregations. This matter was dealt with more directly in 1969.

Questions of racial justice were raised. A suggestion was made that substantial sums be transferred to Black-owned banks. It was regarded as too complex for immediate action. A delegation was sent to Washington by the Conference with a declaration concerning human rights as part of the Washington Witness in 1964, the year the Civil Rights Act for racial justice as passed by Congress.

Christian Education was another concern of this period. In general, it can be said that there was greater unity in this than was found in many of the other tasks. The curriculum was approved. Camps were improved, and programs enriched. Pilgrim Park, Tower Hill and Merom Institute were among those benefiting from improvements. A Long-Range Planning Committee was appointed in March 1967. In November, the project Toward Responsible Freedom was started in cooperation with the Community Renewal Society in response to the plight of the Blacks and poor in Chicago. It was clear that another set of opportunities were taking an important place in the life of the Illinois Conference.

VIII

At the Annual Meeting, June 12, 1968, William Rest expressed his views concerning the next step in the life and work of the Illinois Conference. He said, "With the new emphasis on Race and Peace, we are steering a new course. I am not eligible for a third term. I feel that the man who is responsible for the new direction should be a person who can start with the new course, and stay until its completion. This Fall I am celebrating my 65th birthday which is considered 'Retirement Age' by many in the church ... I, therefore, wish to formally submit my resignation as Conference Minister, to be effective the day before my successor assumes office ... hopefully within the first few months of 1969." However, unexpected changes in William Rest's health compelled a more rapid change. Due to illness he was relieved of his duties August 8, 1968, and the Rev. Hugo Leinberger became Acting Conference Minister, a position changed to Interim Conference Minister after Rest's death a few days later. It was Leinberger's task to carry on the work of the Conference until a new Conference Minister took over eight months later.

IX

The report of the Long-Range Planning Committee had been presented to the Conference by its chair, Rev. Frederick R Trost. He admitted that "we do not have all the answers ... our committee has no set of earth shaking proposals to make." Among the ideas expressed were these: (1) we need to develop cooperative forms of ministry in both rural and urban regions, (2) the need to develop highly skilled specialist to experiment in new forms of ministry (3) that technical and financial resources of the church, if requested by the people of the ghetto, be offered up for immediate investment, (4) openness to new ideas and thought in attempting to understand what God may be saying to us through the events of our time, and (5) faithfulness to the Word in the present hour of history requires stewardship of time, ability, and funds.

After William Rest's resignation was officially accepted, the Conference proceeded with a discussion of the future programs to which he referred. It was voted to designate the national crises — white racism and peace — the first priority of the Conference. There was great difference of opinion as to how to carry out this priority. It was decided to change the order of the day so the delegates could meet in small groups to discuss the proposals, and seek ways to carry out this mission.

The problems felt by members of small churches was brought to the attention of the conference Board by the Wabash Association at its meeting in March 1969. The resolution from the Southeast part of the Conference was quite explicit: "There seems to be a growing dissatisfaction within the Conference, much of which is created because of discrimination against the smaller churches." Previous requests that many events should be held closer had been ignored. As a result, "an individual from this area must expend five to six times as much energy and a comparable period of time to attend meetings convenient to the larger churches." It was requested that the Board of Directors change the by-laws that those churches which had paid their per capita be granted more adequate funds for their expenses in attending meetings. The Executive Committee delayed action until its next meeting. This problem remained unsolved.

In the same month the Board of Directors held a meeting with Directors of the Community Renewal Society to solve some of the problems felt by churches uneasy with the social action ministry being carried on. The following resolution was passed on the first step of solving this problem:

> It is important to know and trust one another. *Expanding Horizons* will be used to communicate the problem of CRS. CRS would like to be on the agenda of the Conference Board meetings.

These problems were on the road to suitable solutions. In his report on Racial Justice, Rev. Alfred E. Williams Jr. concluded that "There is lack of willingness to tackle this problem, not a lack of money." However, finances were weakened by these controversies. *Expanding Horizons* was to be issued six times a year instead of nine, a change which would make $7,000 available for other work.

Something of the wider scene in which the Conference operated can be seen in the resolutions which were adopted during these years. They included, of course, questions of race and peace, Vietnam, and Chicago's handling of the disturbances during the Democratic Convention of 1968. Family planning and the proposed prayer amendment to the constitution were also the subject of resolutions. A program to help world hunger was adopted. The young Conference was concerned with its wider mission as well as its inner organization.

The Rest years were ones in which the Illinois Conference of the United Church of Christ had to find its identity, discover its mission, work out its organization, and secure suitable leadership for its many-sided tasks. With those problems sufficiently taken care of, it was felt that the mission of the Conference could be carried forward effectively. In this report as Interim Conference Minister, Rev. Hugo Leinberger expressed his appreciation for those who had aided him during the interim period, and added these concerns for the future which lay ahead for the Conference.

1. The need to re-examine our structure and our constitution.
2. A task force for the new constitution for the state of Illinois.
3. Counseling and service training programs for the clergy.

New Pathways
THE ADMINISTRATION OF ERSTON M. BUTTERFIELD 1969-1974

There were clearly changes to be made in the Illinois Conference when Rev. Erston M. Butterfield became the second Conference Minister July 1, 1969. He brought with him broader experience in Conference leadership than many, but, on the other hand, it required time to get to know the people and the problems confronting the young Conference.

The volatile problems of the '60s were not confined to Illinois, but there were some aspects which did create special problems in the state. As one leader put it: "Any of us serving in the city during those years remembers the riots spawned by poverty, injustice and the murder of Dr. Martin Luther King Jr. just before Palm Sunday in 1968. At some moments the Church was weak and completely ineffective when it came to its ministry of reconciliation, and at other times the Church was present with its vocation." Rev. Hugo Leinberger's response to the Chicago's handling of the disturbances during the 1968 Democratic Convention was that the UCC would hold no meetings in Illinois until changes were made.

In addition there were problems created by vast differences within the Conference, especially those created by very different ways of life, i.e., contrasting cultures of metropolitan Chicago and downstate. Understanding of the mission and witness of the church were so different as to create problems within the fold. The situation was graphically summed up by the Conference Minister of another state regarding Butterfield's change of position: "From the biggest and most unwieldy Conference in the United Church of Christ to the hottest is a change only a brave man would make ... I hope you noticed that I specifically avoided the use of either word 'frying pan' or the word 'fire'."

I

Erston M. Butterfield, a native of Michigan, had been president of the Michigan Pilgrim Fellowship and delegate to the North American Christian Youth Council and the National Council of Pilgrim Fellowship. After graduation from the University of Michigan and the Oberlin Graduate School of Theology, he served as a teacher, and then Boys' Work Secretary for the YMCA. After serving churches in Ohio, Butterfield was called to conference work. His positions included: Minister and Assistant Superintendent of the Ohio C.C. Conference (1948-52), Minister and Superintendent of the Southeast Conference of C.C. Churches (1953-57), Executive Secretary of the Congregational Union of Cleveland (1957-62), Minister and Superintendent of the Ohio Conference of C.C. Churches (1962-63), and President of the Ohio Conference of the United Church of Christ (1963-69). After coming to Illinois, Butterfield served as president of the Illinois Council of Churches.

The first emphasis of the new Conference Minister was to get acquainted. "My first objective, he said, "was to raise the level of trust and gain a deeper commitment to the total Church at all levels. Taking advantage of the new relationships, staff meetings with ministers were 'listening sessions' to discover feelings and needs, hopes and dreams of professionals who set the spiritual tone in their congregations. Our oneness under the guidance of the Holy Spirit was the informal theme of every meeting." The tone of the new administration was set and carried on in a pastoral spirit seeking to bind the Conference together and improve the moral, of all concerned.

II

It was recognized that the future effectiveness of the Conference would require changes in organization and staff. A series of events in 1969 point out something of the problems and the state of flux prevalent at that time. In June, Rev. Fred Traut, speaking for the Chicago Metropolitan Association, recently changed in name from Northeast Association, proposed to the Board of Directors that CMA would be more effective if it became a separate conference. This proposal was voted down. In July, a committee was formed to define staff relationships and promote greater understanding and smoother cooperation. In September Butterfield requested the creation of a Task Force on Mission and Structure. In October the Conference Minister reported that after 23 group meetings with ministers it was clear this was not the time to restaff. In November the Board of Directors voted not to terminate the position of two staff members who had been given the opportunity to resign in September. A manual of office procedures was issued December 1, 1969.

The Task Force on Mission and Structure was appointed October 23, 1969, with Rev. Keith Torney as chairperson. The situation was described in a resolution of the board of Directors:

> During the time the Task Force is at work the present staff will continue its service to the Conference subject only to necessary reassignment of responsibilities as may be required by interim leadership needs and as determined by the Conference Minister with the approval of the Executive Committee (November 13, 1969).

Meanwhile the finances were suffering. In September the gifts of the Conference were $57,065 short of the goal that had been set. According to the Board minutes, by February 12, 1970 "the Board again faced the distressing financial picture, the budget report showing spending in excess of income, the reduction of reserve funds, the necessity to reduce expenditures in as many areas as possible even to the point of drastically reducing staff by as many as five members, and the need to face all these facts realistically."

The seventh annual meeting of the Illinois Conference took seriously Hugo Leinberger's advice to "re-examine our structure and constitution" and adopted a new structure. The chief feature was the Mission Council, small groups of churches in proximity within the present Associations intended to involve local churches more directly in the Conference and Association program development. The new Mission Councils were to have a voice in both budget and program decisions and enable local churches to have more voice. *Expanding Horizons* reported: "A further responsibility will be the development of mission programs within their own boundaries, possibly on an ecumenical basis." This meeting also held some joint sessions with the United Presbyterian Synod, which was already operating in the Mission Council model. A committee chaired by Rev. Thompson S. Sampson proposed an alternative plan for smaller associations but it was voted down.

This reorganization of the Conference not only resulted in greatly increased program input by the Associations but also in the elimination of several Conference staff positions. A closer relationship between the two levels was assured by having Association Moderators serve on the Conference Council.

The Conference Minister was given primary responsibility under the supervision of the Conference Council to supervise the reorganization of the Conference in its relationship with the Associations. The latter group was to take on more of the program work that had previously been carried on at the Conference level. The Council set the directional goals at its meeting at the beginning of 1974. These included: (1) strengthening local congregations, (2) increasing mission resources, (3) influencing social policy, (4) encouraging unity in diversity, and (5) fulfilling constitutional responsibilities. There was to be continued emphasis on decentralization, planning, evaluation, and administration.

III

A vital part of the program concerned information to all the churches. In May 1969 a reader survey was included in *Expanding Horizons*. This publication had proved to be too expensive. The number of issues had already been reduced and in 1973 *The Pastor's Newsletter* made its appearance, and provided information about the Conference, its programs, people and churches for the next two years. The first issue of *Illinois News* was issued in May 1975.

Another project in the communication area was described by Erston Butterfield: "As part of the 'uniting process,' I developed a colored slide set entitled 'TOGETHER IN MISSION'." Adaptations were made for each of the four Associations, and covered the total mission of the UCC, locally, within the Association, Conference, national and worldwide. This was shown to most of the churches in the Fall of 1970 and the Spring of 1971, and helped greatly in binding us together and in raising OCWM giving in many of the congregations."

IV

The camping program had caused problems and friction. It had been recommended that the Tower Hill and Pilgrim Park properties be sold. Instead, the camps were placed under the management of the Associations in November 1970. East Bay Camp, often used by Christian Education meetings as well as other functions, was placed under the Central Association. Tower Hill was placed under the Chicago Metropolitan Association. The Northern Association was given charge of Pilgrim Park. Merom, where some meetings were held, was owned by the Kentucky-Indiana Conference.

Rev. Clarence M. Higgins Jr., who came to the Illinois Conference in 1971, described some of the changes in program and facilities. As Program Director of the Northern Association he recalls: "The renovation was structural as well as programmatic. We had a dream that the camp (Pilgrim Park) could be the center for renewal in the midst of a very beautiful setting. The camp is now a year-round facility. Bill and Martha Dupree were the camp managers when I arrived and without them the camp would not be there now. An incredible amount of volunteer labor was given to renovate the camp and to build additional structures." Similar changes took place at other camps. Rev. Keith Torney refers to the wider significance of the camping program when he wrote: "it was the camps that pulled our Associations together." The scars of earlier conflict were healed.

V

One of the major emphasis of the years 1969-1976 was the Peace Priority. It was the Viet Nam War period and it was inevitable that the Peace Priority would take on the pressing issues of the time as it sought to define and carry out its task. The need to end war, the size of the defense budget, draft counseling, and the larger questions of the escalation of conventional and nuclear arms were all on the agenda. It aimed at building a constituency from among the churches and keeping "peace education and action" permanently in the Church's mission. The Shalom curriculum was developed by an inter-denominational group know as JED, Joint Educational Development.

A Peace and International Relations Committee (PIRC) was formed to work largely within the Chicago metropolitan area. Roos, the director stated, "The long-range goal we took was that of ending war, of working toward a world in which war is no longer legitimized, sanctioned, and morally acceptable to humankind." PIRC was discontinued after seven years, but its work has been carried on.

The CMA, as part of the Conference, cooperated in a major project, Churches in Transition, with the Community Renewal Society. This effort "to aid churches in racially transitional and pre-transitional communities of metropolitan Chicago to the end that significant and continuing Christian presence and witness will be made by the United Church of Christ and through this presence and witness contributions will be made to the maintenance and development of healthy communities." Rev. Walter E. Ziegenhals originated the program and was in charge of it. As one of the pastors serving a Chicago church at that time wrote, "Many of us looked to the Chicago City Missionary Society (Community Renewal Society) under the leadership of Don Benedict to help us understand the depth of the needs in the city." Benedict and Ziegenhals had been partners in urban mission in New York City and Cleveland prior to coming to Chicago.

VI

In March 1974, Erston Butterfield tendered his resignation as Conference Minister in order to accept a call to a church in Milwaukee. August Burkhardt was called as Interim Conference Minister April 3, 1974. As a layman he had served as Secretary of the Department of Church Building and Finance, United Church Board of Homeland Ministries, and more recently as Interim Superintendent of the Florida Conference. In accepting the call, Burkhardt wrote:

> Every possible effort will be made on my part, during this interim period, to cooperate with you, the Conference Council and the Staff in carrying forward the planned program of the Conference.
>
> Needless to say, this assignment is a real challenge and it is our hope that as partners with the total membership of the Illinois Conference of the United Church of Christ, we, too, may leave a few worthwhile footprints in the sands of time in the Conference — that may be rewarding to all concerned.

Burkhardt served as Interim Minister until the day after Thanksgiving 1974. Writing in the *Pastors' Newsletter,* John B. Muir wrote, "We found a man who is a deeply committed Christian, a knowledgeable churchman, a good listener, a fabulous story-teller and a good administrator. His sense of humor will be legendary among us." After this brief and appreciated interim, the Illinois Conference prepared to begin a new chapter under the leadership of its third Conference Minister.

Creating A Conference Family
THE ADMINISTRATION OF W. STERLING CARY 1975-

The creation of the Illinois Conference was partially completed during its first ten years. The diversity within the state and churches from very different organizational and theological backgrounds had created problems which by 1975 were on the road to solution. The general Conference structure was taken care of during the first few years. The formation of Mission Councils within the Associations were areas of emphasis during the second five years.

However, the situation was far from complete solution when Rev. Dr. W. Sterling Cary assumed the position of Conference Minister in January 1975. He saw his first and continuing task as the creation of a sense of belonging among the churches, therefore the idea of one Conference family became the theme for his administration. Dr. Cary spearheaded an effort to make visits to a large number of rural and small town churches where many felt that the metropolitan area overshadowed them, even left them out in the cold.

Primary responsibility for programing had been moved from the Conference level to the Associations, and changing staff titles from Association Ministers to Associate Conference Ministers was a visible indication of the change in emphasis. During the decade of the '70s all members of the staff were encouraged to visit local churches and endeavor to create a feeling of solidarity among the many churches of the Conference.

I

Rev. W. Sterling Cary was elected Conference Minister at a special meeting September 14, 1974. He assumed his new duties in January 1975, and was officially installed by the Conference on June 10, 1975. In his statement to the Conference just prior to installation, Cary said:

"The mission of the Church in the seventies is that of being a caring community totally immersed in the universal human struggle for fullness of life.

This it seems to me is the mission of the United Church of Christ in the State of Illinois. All of our programs, activity and debating should reflect our determination to concretize our love in a world of desperate need."

Arline Bernard, President of the Illinois Conference, wrote in *The Pastor's Newsletter* concerning Cary, "... a leader who has determination and sticks to programs and situations ... who is able to organize work and delegate responsibilities." The new administration was to be carried on in such a manner.

W. Sterling Cary came to the Illinois Conference from New York City where he was Chief Executive for the Metropolitan and Suffolk Association and Associate Executive of the New York Conference. The previous year he had been elected President of the National Council of Churches. A native of New Jersey and graduate of Morehouse College in Atlanta and Union Theological Seminary in New York, he had served churches in Ohio and New York. Cary had also served on the United Church of Christ Council for Christian Social Action and the Commission for Racial Justice.

II

The words, determination, organization, and delegation, took on specific meanings as the Illinois Conference carried on its ministry. Cary saw as his primary task the development of one team for the whole Conference. His second task, as Cary pointed out to the Executive Council toward the close of his first years, was to meet the expectations of 350 local churches. A year later a Spring Retreat was held for the Association and Conference Councils in an effort to meet, in Cary's words, the "need for the family to talk face to face in order to establish better communication and to share our vision."

In June 1976 the Conference Minister stated that both the Conference and the Associations should be strengthened without weakening either. The meeting of the Conference Council in September illustrated the differing concerns of each of the Associations. Wabash wanted a workshop on stewardship. Northern's concerns were to hold up the vision to which our Lord calls us in the midst of present chaos OCWM, hunger, continuing education for the clergy, etc. CMA expressed the desire to encourage responsible freedom in local churches. Central wanted (1) fiscal responsibility, (2) to overcome areas of conflict between Association and Conference responsibilities and (3) the Conference to be visible to the local church. There was still a long way to go before Cary's vision of a Conference family would be realized. Jean Cleland, Conference President, charged the Executive Council "not to succumb to despair."

A dual foundation had to be laid in order to proceed with the task. One was organization; the other, information. The wide diversity of people, communities and churches still rendered it difficult to develop solidarity within the Illinois Conference. It required time for growth, a development taken into consideration in carrying on such matters as budget planning, balanced representation of women, Blacks and Hispanics, urban and outdoor ministries, ministerial needs, health services, and participation in the wider ministry dealing with world hunger and peace. The tasks had to be unified on four levels, local churches, Mission Councils, Associations and the Conference. The limited understanding of each other' needs, and the complexity and diversity of those needs, further complicated the situation. Like most families, the "Conference Family" was a goal more easily named than created. Steps were started toward the building of a feeling of kinship. The change in title of Association Ministers to Associate Conference Ministers in 1978 was an indication of the move in that direction.

The purpose of the Spring Retreat of Association and Conference Councils was to establish better communication and to share the vision. Another step was taken when a staff member was assigned to relate to each Mission Council. Preparation of the Conference budget, involving as it did the needs and program of the whole Conference and each of the Associations, required new procedures. Meetings were held over a period of several days. Representatives of each unit received requests from each of the areas, then held several meetings to iron out the differences in terms of what was regarded as likely income. After approval of the Conference Council the proposed budget would then be presented to the annual meeting of the Conference for final action.

Every member of the Conference staff made a personal contribution on the basis of each one's personal qualifications and experience. The Conference Council approved a staff deployment plan March 3, 1978. In 1980, Rev. J. Robert Sandman succeeded Rev. Al Williams as Associate Conference Minister-at-Large, a position described as chief administrative assistant and coordinator of program, continuing education and resource person for staff and clergy with special responsibility for church development.

III

Stewardship became the top priority of the Conference in 1978 and the Rev. Donald S. Stoner was called as Associate Conference Minister for Stewardship. In carrying out this project the publication of *Focus* made its appearance. Its function was described by the Conference Minister: "FOCUS, our new Conference publication, will be providing direction and resources for interpreting and strengthening our common ministry of servanthood through the church." Two years later Stewardship Workshops were held throughout the Conference.

The Hinsdale property was sold in 1983 and the Conference headquarters was moved to Westchester. In August Rev. Jeffrey N. Stinehelfer assumed the duties of Associate Conference Minister for Stewardship and Interpretation, and Rev. William Voelkel succeeded Rev. Fred Traut as Associate Conference Minister for the Chicago Metropolitan Association. The covenant with the Community Renewal Society was renewed, and *Illinois Focus* was to expand its coverage from largely stewardship matters to include all the concerns of the Conference. A five-year stewardship program was adopted in 1984.

The tenth annual report of the Conference Minister summarized progress to date: "Ten years ago the upstate-downstate separation was constantly evidenced. Now on all levels there are reflections of acceptance of joint responsibility for the life of the whole Conference. A few areas where this is being shown are through our relationships with the UCC affiliated institutions and agencies: the covenant relationship with the Community Renewal Society, the outdoor ministry program, OCWM support, covenantal relationship between local churches, our response to world needs. We call upon the delegates and visitors to continue to be actively responsive to the needs in all areas of church life that we can in fact become the Body of Christ. (May 31, 1984)

IV

One of the major concerns of our nation in recent years has been the position of women in a working society. The Illinois Conference has made a major contribution to this question by encouraging women clergy. The growing number of women ministers was a factor in the establishment of the Women's Resource Team. This opportunity for strengthening and enriching the Church's ministry has been an important emphasis.

The number of women among the Conference clergy has increased dramatically in the decade of the '80s. In 1981 there were 22 women serving churches in the Conference. Of these, 15 were ordained. Only six years later, the number of women clergy had increased to 208, of whom 54 were serving local churches, and 3 on the Conference staff.

In 1984 the following resolution was adopted: "Resolved that search committees of local churches covenant with Conference staff to consider seriously women candidates when pulpits are vacant; and further to utilize women as pulpit supplies and interims. This priority shall be implemented through staff initiative and support and through the work of the Association Church and Ministry Committees." It was further stated that by 1990 at least three full-time staff members be women, lay or ordained.

It is much easier to carry out this mission on the Conference and Association levels than in local churches. Women's early service was in limited areas associated with the traditional women's role. Thus Marguerite Davison was assigned as secretary to the Women's Fellowship in Congregational Christian churches prior to the merger. Christian Education was another area to which it was comparatively easy to call women. Rev. Clara Spencer began this service in 1964. The following year Mrs. Ethel Winsor became an Interim Director. Madeline F. Bach was called to the assignment of Adult Education in 1960, becoming one of the staff members of the Division of Parish Life two years later. Mrs. Pauline E. Gallup was Conference Treasurer 1985-1987.

Each of the Associations has had women on its staff. Wabash Association, which joined Central in 1989, has had two pastors-at-large: Rev. Myrtle Beafont (1968) and Rev. Carolyn F. Welch (1976-1979). Northern Association called Rev. Lavon Bayler in 1980 as Area Minister. Chicago Metropolitan Association has had as Interim Area Ministers, Rev. Nancy Jo Kemper (1983-1984), and Rev. Elizabeth Bacon (1985). The Rev. Karen Olm-Stolting became area minister in 1988 in Central.

In this connection it should be noted that women have long held elective positions of leadership in the Illinois Conference. Since 1974 six have served as Conference Presidents: Mrs. Arline Bernard, Mrs. Jean Cleland, Mrs. Helen Heimburger, Rev. Harriett N. Martin, Rev. Christine D. Barton and Mrs. Elizabeth Kingsbury. Two of them had served as vice-presidents. Nine of the fourteen individuals who have served as secretary since 1964 have been women: Mrs. R.K. Wobbe, Mrs. J.P. Richmond, Mrs. Frank C. Green, Mrs. Gilbert Horn, Rev. Sally T. Scheib, Mrs. Helen Heimberger, Mrs. Julie M. Ullman, Mrs. Patricia Kitner and Ms. Dorothy Auw. Men have also served as secretary, notably Rev. Dean C. Plassmann, Rev. George Hirst, Rev. Joel Rief, Rev. Lawrence J. Rezash, and Rev. Robert C. Ahrendt. Ann Benedict was selected as the Conference representative on the ERA Committee.

It is well known that a great deal of the work of the Conference and Associations — program, information, supplies, public relations and personal contact with churches and the general public — has been handled extremely well by women. These tasks have been carried on under various titles, such as registrar, year book secretary, audio-visual librarian, assistant secretary, assistant treasurer, office manager, and so on. Those who have filled these important positions of responsibility are so numerous that they must be included in the appendices. However, it should not be overlooked that these individuals have made the better publicized aspects of the Conference work and history possible.

V

The Illinois Conference has been increasingly inclusive and has served all races and many national and ethnic groups as they have become residents in the state. Members of many groups for whom ministry had been provided have become leaders in all levels of the United Church of Christ. By way of illustration, in the middle of the last century some churches, such as the one in Byron, were stations in the underground railroad. In 1909 Lincoln Memorial Congregational Church was founded by a group of black business and professional men who had been educated in schools and colleges founded by the American Missionary Society. Other important UCC churches serving the black population are Church of the Good Shepherd (1924), Park Manor (1953) and Trinity (1962). Many from these backgrounds have become leading pastors, conference executives, seminary presidents, and executives in the national instrumentalities of the United Church of Christ. The ministering to minority ethnic groups has made it possible for them to make the transition from the first step to earned leadership much more rapidly.

The diversity of national origin is not new but, with support from the Community Renewal Society, it has been increasing. The Armenian Congregational Church was organized in 1916, and the Assyrian Evangelical United Church of Christ first came on the scene in 1919. In 1948 Christ Church of Chicago was founded by Japanese-Americans. The Korean United Church of Christ began its ministry in 1976 followed by the Korean Yung Saeng church in 1987. The Philippine American Ecumenical Church joined the UCC in 1979, and the Philippine United Church of Christ was organized four years later.

In recent years a large number of Hispanic people have moved into Illinois. The United Church of Christ has received them into its fellowship. The First Spanish United Church of Christ in Chicago was organized in 1961. First Congregational Church of Chicago, organized in 1851, now has a Hispanic congregation. Other Hispanic churches in Chicago are Millard Congregational (1880) and San Lucas UCC (1978). A Hispanic mission church was started in Joliet in 1984. In the same year, the Rev. Dr. Jose de Jesus began his work as Director of Hispanic Ministry in cooperation with the Community Renewal Society. Four years later he was called as Area Conference Minister of the Chicago Metropolitan Association. In 1987 a project for the Center for Ethnic and Coalition Ministries was launched in cooperation with the United Church of Christ for Homeland Ministries and the Community Renewal Society. The Illinois Conference receives members of the human family from every race and nation whose members come into its region, and draws upon their experience and understanding even as it seeks to meet their spiritual needs.

VI

The Illinois Conference also serves people of all ages, meeting the distinctive needs of each group. The programs at Pilgrim Park and Tower Hill camps serve all ages. Both centers have been expanded in recent years, improving facilities and program. Each camp has its own committee and association connections, but they are under a conference committee, the Outdoor Ministry Committee.

The Conference ministry to youth has not been limited to camping experiences. In 1987 a policy was voted to elect youth delegates — individuals age 18 to 24 — for attendance at denominational business meetings. There were 36 youth delegates representing the Illinois Conference at the General Synod in

1985 in Ames, Iowa. The Campus Ministry program has not been limited to making religious programs available to students in institutions of higher learning around the state. Each church has been asked to inform the campus pastors of its youth in colleges and universities so a more personal contact can be made.

In 1981 a Task Force on Aging was established. Workshops were held in a number of churches. Suitable programs to serve this older portion of the Conference membership were discussed and carried on. The facilities for housing and health care under the Health and Human Resources Council of the Illinois Conference will be mentioned separately.

VII

The clergy hold a distinctive place in the life and work of the Conference. Their services are varied and are related to the entire work of the fellowship. Several programs directly meet the needs of the clergy. Theological education comes first in point of time. The three seminaries most closely related to the Illinois Conference are Chicago, United and Eden. These seminaries are aided through CUE (Chicago, United, Eden), an UCC organization established in 1973, not formally a part of the Conference but a channel through which churches can support the work of the seminaries. Of the churches in the Illinois Conference, 48 percent made contributions through CUE.

Continuing Education and Retreats are channels through which ministers are served and strengthened and their ministry enriched. The Professional Association of Clergy, founded in 1974 by a group of UCC clergy, is a voice which speaks for the clergy and provides a wide assortment of information, and is now officially part of the Conference. Special clergy needs such as health, insurance and financial problems are met by committees of the Conference. Retirement years are served in large measure by the Pension Boards, a national instrumentality. Interim Ministry has been receiving renewed attention in recent years. There is always a need for pastors to serve churches as they seek new leadership and prepare for the adjustment required as a new era begins. Its significance and positive potential has been receiving more attention than in previous years. In cooperation with the Disciples of Christ (The Christian Church), the Conference has been active in this area. Some ministers have decided on interim work as their specialty and continued calling.

VIII

The Christian Church in general, and the Illinois Conference of the United Church of Christ in particular, have responded to the momentous changes of the 20th Century in various ways. Rev. Walter Ziegenhals had a vision for a program to assist churches whose communities were undergoing major changes. This Churches In Transition program, sponsored by the Chicago Metropolitan Association was a cooperative venture with the Community Renewal Society and the United Church Board for Homeland Ministries, was largely in Chicago. Rev. Ziegenhals was called to take charge of the Churches In Transition program, his unique vision.

Another project, New Initiative in Church Development, was designed to help establish churches in newly developed areas. The original three-year program, launched in cooperation with the Board for Homeland Ministries, received support of 180 churches in the Conference. Those established were more diverse than the ones in the Churches in Transition program, and included suburban settings and were scattered geographically.

The Outdoor Ministry program, adopted in 1980, included people of all ages and, therefore, was a departure from the traditional youth-oriented camping programs which had been part of the Conference work for many years. The Pilgrim Park and Tower Hill committees continued to manage their respective camps, but the costs for the Camping Committees were provided for in the Conference budget. The task for the Outdoor Ministry Committee was to coordinate the work of the two committees and affirm this ministry as a continuing priority of the Conference. Expansion of both camps and a successful major fund-raising campaign for Tower Hill were among the accomplishments of this period.

In 1980 a new approach to Conference ministry began with the appointment of the Task Force in Fellowship in the Arts. Its purpose was: (1) to act as an advocate of the Arts, the artist and the creative life of all through involvement with local churches, the Associations and the Conference; (2) To promote dialogue between faith and the arts; (3) To encourage and strengthen our faith through the arts and creative activities in our personal and corporate lives; (4) To provide opportunities for sharing various skills and modes of ministry in the arts; (5) To provide opportunities for fellowship and mutual support among people involved with or concerned about the arts; and (6) To develop a network through which information and resources can be shared. The Illinois Fellowship in the Arts has by no means been limited to a small group within the state. Rev. Carla Gilbert, national president of the UCCFA (United Church of Christ Fellowship in the Arts) stated, "Without Illinois, we just wouldn't have had any official presence" at a national meeting. Works of Illinois artists were bought by the Des Moines Presbytery and a Roman Catholic group at a national event in Virginia. In 1985 "some visitors from East and West Germany were given drawings by Laini Zinn of Lacon as a token of world Christian fellowship." Displays at General Synod 17 included a quilt made by three members of whom one was UCCFA advisory board member L. Zinn.

IX

The Ministry and Mission Working Group was formed as an addition to the Conference Council to coordinate the work of several groups. The Outdoor Ministry, the Professional Association of Clergy and the Fellowship of the Arts were included in its task. The audio visual library was also part of its work. Its assignment has been to increase the effectiveness and availability of important aids for the Church's program. Recently cooperation with a similar program of the Disciples of Christ has expanded it greatly. This working group has also been assigned the task of coordinating the programs of the Association Church and Ministry Committees, and the Family Life Consultation and the Women's Resource Team and the Youth Ministry.

The Public Witness Working Group consists of representatives of each of the Associations and the Community Renewal Society. Concerned primarily with the resolution process, it has advised the Conference Council in many matters of public policy and social action. The work of the Justice and Peace network is reported by them. In this same connection, staff and other members of the Illinois Conference have visited other places and brought back reports of conditions which require support of the churches of the Conference. Among the nations visited are: Syria, Israel, Jordan, East Germany, Hungary, the Philippines, Mexico, Nicaragua, Guatemala, and other Central and South American nations.

The Higher Education/Ecumenical Working Group is concerned with three basic areas: (1) Relations with the Christian Church (Disciples of Christ) in Illinois and Wisconsin, (2) Participation in United Ministries in Higher Education, and (3) Participation in the Illinois Conference of Churches, of which Robert Sandman is currently president.

The work of the Illinois Conference was not limited to its geographical area. In 1975 a program was started to raise $50,000 for India and/or Africa to deal with world hunger. As one of the members of the Conference Council wrote, "This was a loan type of thing for the purchase of seed, fertilizer, etc. ... I don't think other conferences were involved in such."

The Stewardship and Mission Working Group carried on its five-year program initiated in 1984 which includes both education and financial support for missions. Visits to local churches are an important part of its work. Financial support from the Tuthill Fund has been given to various programs, including: Rural Health Program (Philippines), Lucy Perry Noble Institute (India), Evangelical Hospital (India), Tod and Ana Gobledale (South Africa), Missioner-in-Residence Program (Sitholes), UCC Seminar to Africa (Sterling Cary's participation), and Guatemalan refugee relief (Southern Mexico). The Latin American Council of Churches, held in Brazil, was attended by Jose de Jesus. Other work has been supported in Zimbabwe, Ghana and Japan. Bishop Ruiz visited the 1989 annual meetings, and spoke about the Guatemalan relief project in his diocese in Southern Mexico. The mission outreach of the Illinois Conference extends around the world.

The Evangelism/Church Extension Working Group is concerned with both training and church development. A major emphasis has been training in Calling-Caring Ministries. Certified leaders have been trained: five in Northern Association, four in CMA, and three in Central. This group provides financial support for buildings and programs for churches. New churches are given necessary support, and are moved to self-support as soon as possible, thus enabling the Conference to help in other places. Churches of Promise, and Illinois Growth and Development Program was a major new thrust in 1983-87. One hundred thirty-eight churches agreed to participate in a two-year membership development program. Training sessions were led by Rev. James Bidle, Rev. Alan Johnson, and Rev. Henry Simmons of the staff of the Board for Homeland Ministries.

Christian Education has always been a concern of the churches; therefore, of the Conference, too. When the new UCC curriculum was introduced, workshops were held in each Association, and consultants were made available to local churches. Among those services provided were Christian Education Retreats and Training Workshops. At least portions of the curriculum were being used in 145 churches by 1984. Another program was carried on by LAMP, advanced training for adults in response to the new category of Licensed Ministry adopted by the General Synod in 1983. The annual gathering of the Great Lakes Association of Educators is held each year in Illinois, at Techny Tower.

The Conference introduced a somewhat new emphasis in 1988, called Environmental Stewardship. The introduction to the resolution proceeding its adoption states: "God's command to humanity is the responsibility to keep the creative process alive, not the destruction of the process, to live in the image of God as creator for the good of the whole creation, both now and into the future." It calls upon the Church to face the problems of pollution of air and water, and to promote recycling. In both its purchases and in its teachings, the Conference takes seriously the pressing problems of the earth today.

The Illinois Conference of the United Church of Christ has all the mechanisms in place for its many members and churches to work together in areas of Christian service and growth.

The Associations of the Illinois Conference

Each of the Associations is a significant part of the Illinois Conference and has its own special ministry. Many programs of the Conference are carried on through them. Minister's training, ordination, standing, and assistance with placement are done at this level of the organization. Beyond that, each Association serves in a different area, and each adapts its work to the needs and opportunities of its particular region.

Central Association consists of 62 churches. It is located largely in a rich agricultural region, but each of its five Mission Councils contains at least one church in one of the larger cities, i.e. those with populations from 35,000 to 125,000 in its territory. Central covers a region 300 miles from east to west, and 150 miles from north to south. Although the churches are largely rural and small town groups they are all easily accessible to the larger churches. The program of Central is attuned to its region. Early staff members were Rev. Louis N. Lammert, Rev. William Halfafker, Rev. J. Robert Sandman and Rev. Charles D. Hindman. From 1984 to 1989, Rev. C. Arthur Bradley, Rev. C. Thomas Jackson and Rev. Karen Olm-Stoelting, have served Wabash Association as well as Central.

In 1984, Central Association launched a five year program with three goals: communication, identity and spirituality. Pastoral Assistance teams greatly increased the ability of ministers and churches to work together and resolve conflict. Workshops were held through LEAD (Leadership Training and Development) to train members to call on others. Bradley reported that "a two and a half year task force worked on discovering that we have within the UCC a common vision which could be projected, although it would include widely divergent understandings of Christian morality, Biblical revelation, and ministry to the world."

The breadth of Central Association's program can be seen in the existence of two very different projects. The Missioner-in-Residence project brought into the churches people actively engaged in the world-wide mission of the United Church of Christ. The People of the Land project dealt directly with the religious needs of the many churches and people facing the serious problems met daily by those engaged in agricultural work in the area. Both were carried out in cooperation with the Northern Association. This undertaking also brought the youth into the main stream of the Association.

The Chicago Metropolitan Association was first called North East since that was the section of Illinois which it served. It includes 166 churches located in nine Mission Councils. It is, in fact, far more varied in its churches and communities than the name suggests. For instance, Immanuel UCC at Papineau and the United Church of Chebanse, the most southerly in CMA, and the churches in Waukegan on the northern extreme bear little resemblance to the wide variety of communities within Chicago itself. The CMA has nine Mission Councils. Chicago churches are members of six of the Mission Councils, each of which includes some suburban churches. Three Mission Councils contain only congregations outside of Chicago.

Mention has been made of some of the work being carried on through the CMA branch of the Illinois Conference. The great influx of people from other places, a constant feature of the city life, has been assisted by other organizations. The most prominent partner has been the Community Renewal Society, known many years ago as the Chicago Congregational Union and the Chicago City Missionary Society. The Church in Transition project and that concerned with Ethnic Ministry are the most prominent undertakings. Leaders in these ministries have included not only the Associate Conference Ministers, Rev. Fred Traut and Rev. William Voekel; the Area Conference Ministers, Rev. Delbert Schrag (for whom a building is named at Tower Hill), Rev. Jimmie Sawyer and Rev. Jose de Jesus; but also leaders of the Community Renewal Associety, Rev. Donald J. Benedict, Rev. Paul Sherry, Rev. Walter Ziegenhals and Rev. Bennie Whiten, to name but a few. A great many members of many churches carry on these various ministries on boards, committees and other channels.

Other emphases on CMA have included special training for interim ministers, placement of women in pastorates, and guidance for those preparing for the ministry. Chicago Metropolitan Association, has, or instance, more "in-care" people than any other association in the United Church of Christ. The Mission Design, a plan adopted in 1983 included provision for a capital fund campaign for improvement and expansion at Tower Hill Camp and major funds for CRS.

CMA works with other groups in several important areas. The South Side Health Project involves, in addition to the Association, the Community Renewal Society, Elmhurst College, Chicago Theological Seminary, the Evangelical Health Systems and Life Link. Another enterprise is the Interfaith Council for the Homeless. Meetings are held with the Disciples and the Chicago Presbytery in an effort to expand the ministry of all three groups. The Associate Conference Minister is part of the group of religious leaders working together in metropolitan Chicago.

The Northern Association, located roughly west of the Fox River and north of the Illinois River, consists of 91 churches participating in eight Mission Councils. The area includes two large cities, the Quad Cities and Rockford, some suburban communities, many small towns and much rural area. Its work requires great variety of program as it carries on its mission in the Illinois Conference. As Robert C. Meissner wrote in the 1988 report: "... economically and culturally diverse. We are an Association of small, medium and large churches, extending from rural hamlets to urban sprawl."

An Association of such diversity requires many types of program. Northern decided that youth should become members of all committees and workshops as well as of the Conference Council. Pilgrim Park has been improved and enlarged. Programs there are available for all generations. Workshops and Retreats have been major programs of Northern. Subjects have included Christian Education, Spiritual Growth, Church Planning, Peace Priority and Hunger, and Women's Spring Celebration. CAML (Church of Accredited Ministering Laypeople), a series of three-weekend study experiences for laypeople, has also been a part of its program as well as Mission Possible Workshops.

Problems within the area, such as the crisis in agriculture and unemployment in the largest cities have been faced. The Association included in its ministry the Urban Mission in the Quad Cities and special ministry to prisoners in the Rockford jail. The Fox Valley was the site of a new church start. Northern Association, however, has not limited its attention to its own geographical area. The Missioner-in-Residence program has been included in cooperation with Central Association. Area Conference Minister Rev. Lavon Bayler visited India and was in touch with mission work there.

Rev. James B. Stinehelfer was Associate Conference Minister in 1964-1966 and was followed by Rev. Edwin J. Hoefer in 1967-1978. The next Association Conference Minister was Rev. Clarence M. "Clip" Higgins (who as a retreat house and center named for him at Pilgrim Park), who served from 1978 to 1986, and most recently is Rev. Robert C. Meissner. Rev. Higgins had served as Program Director and then Area Minister in the period from 1971-1978 and then was succeeded as Area Minister by Rev. Lavon Bayler. With a limited staff, it has been clear, as it has been with all the Associations, that the work has been made possible by a large number of persons, lay and clerical, who are not members of the staff.

The Wabash Association, originally called South East, was located in that section of the state, and consisted of only ten churches when it voted in 1989 to become a Mission Council of Central Association. These churches date from the Wabash Christian Conference which was established in 1819. In its largely agricultural region, economic problems such as unemployment ranging from 18 percent to 25 percent in 1985, forced large numbers, especially younger ones, to move.

For many years Wabash was served by pastors of some of its churches a part-time pastors-at-large. In order of service, these were: Rev. Clare B. Nave, Rev.

Donald R. Scott, Rev. William L. Halfaker, Rev. J. David Thompson, Rev. Carolyn F. Welsh and Rev. Glenn A. Gettinger. Since 1984 staff members of Central Association have served as liaison with the Illinois Conference. Two meetings were held annually, one informational, the other, inspirational. The Small Church Workshop held in 1988 was an illustration of one, and programs featuring missionaries, singspiration and evangelists were of the other type. Clusters were another feature of its ministry — encouraging churches in the same geographical area to work together in program, outreach and mission.

This Association, many miles from other portions of the Illinois Conference, became a Mission Council of Central Association in 1989, and soon after, six of its churches withdrew from the UCC, and the other four joined the Indiana-Kentucky Conference. The remaining Associations are definitely active and important members of the Illinois Conference family.

THE EXTENDED FAMILY

The Conference family consists of far more than those within the Churches, Mission Councils, Associations and Conference. The Directory of the Illinois Conference lists 22 church-related institutions and 42 church-related agencies.

In many ways the most extensive outreach is the Health and Human Services Council. This was organized in 1983 by the agencies involved. Its purpose was stated: "The purpose of the Council will be to coordinate health and welfare planning and activities of the United Church of Christ related institutions, assist them in evaluating their individual and corporate effectiveness in keeping with the principle as the love of persons with special need, and encourage financing of this program which reflects the uniqueness of the Christian mission."

The Health and Human Services Council includes 11 institutions and 29 agencies. The Council board consists of five persons elected by the Illinois Conference and the remaining members are representatives of the agencies. The care provided helps people from pre-school to the aged, and includes housing, counseling, hospitalization, and facilities for the handicapped. The largest number of facilities are those of the Bensenville Home Society (Life Link Corporation) with seven, and the Evangelical Health Systems and Evangelical Health Corporation with nine. When it became apparent that there was a need for additional health facilities in the south side of Chicago, the Conference joined with the Community Renewal Society and Elmhurst College, CTS, EHS, and the Bensonville Home Society to form the Health and Human Services Group to help meet that need. This group was instrumental in establishing the South Side Health Project.

A second group of related institutions are in the field of education. Two are colleges whose work dates back many years. Illinois College was founded in 1829, and Elmhurst college dates from 1871. Three theological seminaries are closely connected with the Conference, although Eden, founded in 1850, is in Missouri, and United Theological Seminary, founded in 1960, is located in the Twin Cities of Minnesota. The third, Chicago Theological Seminary, accepted its first students, transfers from Andover and Union Seminaries, as seniors in 1858. In 1973 CUE Midwest Seminaries was established, a link between the churches of the region and the seminaries.

As previously mentioned, the Community Renewal Society, an independent body from its founding in 1882, is a partner in work in the Chicago area, and operates Pleasant Valley Outdoor Center in Woodstock. Other related agencies are: Dove, Inc., located in Decatur; Emmaus Homes, an agency for the mentally handicapped, just across the Mississippi in Missouri; and Sunburst Youth Home in Wisconsin. If the Illinois Conference is a family, these institutions and agencies can be considered cousins.

A Quarter Century in Retrospect

A quarter century of history of the Illinois Conference of the United Church of Christ now can be viewed as a portion of the total Christian scene as it has occurred in every place, in every century. This Conference is a microcosm of what the Church has been and done through the centuries.

The twentieth century has been a time of increasing cooperation among the various churches. It has been a time of church unions. Some have been reunions, and some have been the uniting of groups with separate histories. The United Church of Christ, organized in 1957, is a venture of the latter type. These movements toward unity are attempts to outgrow the divisiveness which has been common for at least nine hundred years, the breaking away of one group from another. The reasons for the divisions have usually been cloaked in pious terms. Some reasons have been "religious," other were the result of differing political objectives and still others were because of national and racial differences. Such differences are always part of the human scene, but are contrary to the best in Christian tradition. The scriptural motto of the UCC continues to be "that they all may be one."

There have been breaks in the unity of Christian churches for ecclesiastical and theological reasons, all of them supported by biblical references. Briefly, these reasons concern church organizations, forms of worship, statements of faith, and rules of human conduct. These are always part of the landscape, and have led to the formation of hundreds of denominations. Each of these concerns had its place in the backgrounds of the four pathways that joined in the formation of the Conferences in the United Church of Christ.

The Illinois Conference, like all the others, could not become a happy union by decree. There were major differences in organization. In the early years of the Conference these problems were faced on the Conference level. The second period made a place for the important contributions of smaller units — the Associations and Mission Councils. This opened the way for Churches to become active members of the Conference group. Differences in belief and worship continued, but in time diversity was recognized as a strong pillar of the Conference as it is of any human family.

Just as family members have various personalities, do did the people of the Illinois Conference. In short, such attributes as personality conflicts, bickering, and personal ambition were unavoidable. These were negative aspects of family life to be outgrown before the positive side could become really strong. More readily admitted than the bickering were the differences in communities and areas of the territory. It required time and effort to grow beyond the territory. It required time and effort to grow beyond the negative effect of all these differences.

This quarter century has also admirably demonstrated the strength which comes from practicing what we preach. The Conference became a Christian family by carrying out its mission. In short, ministry to human need is an ever-present source of strength. Many of the needs faced have been within its own territory — urban, suburban and rural projects. The Conference also provides support and leadership for national and worldwide missions. Its membership attends to peace, hunger, poverty and housing. These works served to develop a Christian Conference Family.

After eighteen years of declining membership, the Conference reversed that trend for the first time in 1984. The group is growing, but like most families some members are not active participants. Some churches rarely show up at meetings of Mission Councils, Associations or the Conference, and there are those who do not even report on their year's work that others may rejoice in their successes or provide support when it is needed.

Ever searching for ways to improve, in 1988 the Executive Committee of the Illinois Conference Council engaged Rev. William A. Hulteen, Associate Director for the Great Lakes Region of the Office of Church Life and Leadership of the UCC, to make a study of the relationships of the various partners in the Illinois Conference. He included in his task, local churches, clergy, Mission Councils, Associations, the Conference, and church-related institutions.

In carrying out his assignment Hulteen met with twenty-three conversation groups, which included 237 persons. His report pointed out both strengths and weaknesses. The greatest need seemed to be for the ministers to be more active in informing their members of the work of the Conference. Moreover, the limited number of positions on Boards and Committees adversely affected the amount of active participation in the workings of the conference, and many lost touch with the wider work when their terms expired. When this finding is added to the wide diversity of places and backgrounds within the Conference, it was apparent that better, more effective channels of communication are still needed.

The Illinois Conference has provided exprienced leadership for other Conferences and for the national instrumentalities of the United Church of Christ. Some of its leaders have moved on as Conference Ministers, thereby providing many others with experienced guidance. Among those who have served in Illinois and were called as Conference Ministers are: Rev. James R.

Smucker (Central Pacific and New York), Rev. Alfred E. Williams (Massachusetts), Rev. Clarence M. Higgins Jr. (Nebraska) and Rev. Jeffrey M. Stinehelfer (Minnesota).

Others who were formerly active as pastors in Illinois have been called to serve in other states as Conference Ministers. These include Rev. Charles G. Hoskinson (Missouri), Rev. Frederck R. Trost (Wisconsin), Rev. Clyde H. Miller Jr. (Rocky Mountain) Rev. Curtis Mintes (Vermont), Rev. David Y. Hirano (Connecticut) and Rev. Donald J. Sevetson (Central Pacific).

Illinois has also helped provide experienced leadership on the national level. These include: Rev. Joseph H. Evans, for years Secretary of the UCC; Rev. C. Shelby Rooks, Executive Vice President of the United Church Board of Homeland Ministeries; Rev. Donald L. Stoner, Director of the Planned Giving Program; Rev. Reuben A. Sheares II, Executive Director of the Office for Church Life and Leadership. Rev. Paul W. Sherry was elected President of the United Church of Christ in 1989, following his tenture as Executive Director of the Community Renewal Society. In addition, numerous individuals from the Illinois Conference have served on National Boards and Committees. The Illinois Conference has been a rich source of guidance for the Wider Church.

The Illinois Conference has also cooperated with other groups. Leadership has been provided for the Illinois Conference of Churches, The Church Federation of Greater Chicago, and untold numbers of local church and pastoral organizations. This aspect of the work can be illustrated by the Open Letter to the People of Chicago, Thanksgiving 1988. It is signed by Joseph Cardinal Bernadin, Rabbi Herman Schaalman, and W. Sterling Cary, Conference Minister of the Illinois Conference, UCC. The following portions of the letter could stand as an expression of our statewide mission:

> " ... Interracial and interreligious peace and good will depend on our willingness to work together for the ideals which make us a community. In particular, let us work for those reforms which will end the scandal of widespread poverty in the midst of affluence. The poor among us are our brothers and sisters. There an be no lasting peace in our city while they languish on isolated islands of poverty and despair.
>
> " ... We belong to a wider community. We are Chicagoans. We are members of the same human family. We are children of God. We believe profoundly that the more we work together for a united city, the more we will succeed in achieving justice and peace."

In its 25 years, the Illinois Conference has become a family serving the needs of our region, recognizing that we are all part of God's worldwide human family. Good solid groundwork is now in place to support even greater works by the Illinois Conference of the United Church of Christ in the years to come.

APPENDIX A — STATISTICS

Year	Churches	Members	Church School	Members Added	Members Lost	OCWM	Local Expense	Capital Expenses
1963	148 (E&R)	58,399	30,093	3,462	3,144	579,561	1,316,760	780,383
	227 (CC)	87,486	44,709	6,431	6,691	1,017,836	4,620,229	1,750,518
1964	388	71,295	71,295	9,580	9,934	1,669,407	7,648,328	3,643,500
1965	385	149,267	65,760	9,460	9,827	1,732,672	8,095,365	2,983,687
1966	376	148,672	60,430	9,165	9,446	1,773,267	8,490,886	2,159,218
1967	372	148,257	56,238	8,348	8,761	1,247,383	8,650,265	2,246,113
1968	365	146,965	53,712	8,461	9,934	1,109,783	8,940,257	2,021,285
1969	360	144,084	51,240	7,555	10,269	1,057,238	9,232,912	2,748,868
1970	357	142,781	46,992	7,252	8,592	962,130	9,424,095	2,573,292
1971	350	139,583	43,643	6,803	10,371	889,527	9,801,543	2,095,803
1972	342	137,214	41,901	6,767	8,935	907,392	10,020,622	4,689,434
1973	343	134,951	39,328	6,736	8,764	923,701	10,530,511	1,519,079
1974	340	133,247	36,244	6,949	8,973	948,191	11,670,870	2,197,492
1975	337	131,815	36,222	6,121	7,391	983,145	12,414,710	2,642,191
1976	338	130,850	35,049	5,894	6,494	1,025,529	13,679,500	2,104,775
1977	337	129,198	35,029	6,075	7,653	1,067,766	14,343,050	3,049,391
1978	335	126,165	32,905	5,146	7,213	1,134,220	15,436,220	2,216,118
1979	332	123,832	31,879	5,272	7,118	1,172,588	13,840,418	1,729,214
1980	331	123,547	30,774	5,664	5,665	1,233,858	16,976,008	3,385,081
1981	330	122,236	29,804	5,636	7,118	1,316,452	18,963,438	3,762,271
1982	328	121,603	28,128	5,605	5,899	1,430,496	20,843,352	3,968,139
1983	331	120,930	26,951	5,984	6,395	1,505,106	21,464,354	3,593,880
1984	332	121,293	25,107	5,710	5,295	1,545,600	24,604,228	2,457,756
1985	328	120,210	26,452	5,446	6,430	1,664,412	25,745,485	2,088,194
1986	329	118,576	25,779	4,930	6,537	1,728,246	26,660,513	1,174,510
1987	328	118,729	25,530	5,670	5,108	1,797,577	27,351,801	2,806,507
1988	325	117,597	25,638	4,432	5,579	1,828,439	28,977,373	2,847,751

APPENDIX B: ACTING CONFERENCES 1963-1964

NORTHERN ILLINOIS ACTING CONFERENCE

President: Rev. William L. Rest
Vice-Prsident: Rev. Paul Bloesch
Secretary: Rev. Dean Plassmann
Extension/Urban Strategy: Rev. Hugo Leinberger
Minister of Parish Program: Rev. Louis Lammert
Treasurer: William H. Bobsin
Lay Members-at-Large: Paul Nebold
Frances Mies

CONGREGATIONAL CHRISTIAN ACTING CONFERENCE

Minister and Acting Sup't.: Rev. James R. Smucker
Moderator: Rev. Merrill J.A. Dalrymple
Assistant Moderator: Lee C. Ward
President of Corp and Bd. of Trustees: Rev. Joseph H. Evans
Vice President Trustees and Corp: Rev. Jack Fay Robinson
Treasurer: Harry E. Kellogg
Ass't Treas. and Bookkeeper: Mrs. Opal Moore
and Office Manager
Minister & Assoc. Sup't, Northern Area: Rev. John S. Queen
Minister & Assoc. Sup't., Southern Area: Rev. C. Theodore Roos
Minister of Christian Education: Rev. Robert D. Hotelling
Director of Christian Education: Miss Lucille D. Frost
Director of Christian Stewardship: Russell H. Palmer
Secretary, Women's Fellowship: Miss Marguerte Davision
Interim Director of Urban Mission: Rev. Donald L. Benedict
Consultant: Rev. Frank L. Edwards
Scribe: Rev. Ray S. Steakley
Assistant Scribe: Mrs. Addison M. Hainer
Enrollment Clerk: Mrs. Karl Sheldon
Year Book Editor: Mrs. Robert D. Hotelling
Camp Managers: Pilgrim Park: Rev. William D. Dupree
Tower Hill: Ernest V. Schroeder

APPENDIX C: CONFERENCE STAFF

CONFERENCE MINISTERS

Rev. William L. Rest (1964-1968)
Rev. Hugo Leinberger (Interim, 1968-1969)
Rev. Erston M. Butterfield (1969-1974)
Mr. August Burchardt (Interim, 1974)
Rev. W. Sterling Cary (1975 -)

CONFERENCE OFFICE STAFF

Miss Madeline F. Bach (1966-1969) Adult Education
Rev. Donald L. Benedict (1964-1969) Dir. for Urban Mission
Mr. Arthur C. Borch (1967-69) Ass't Treas./Business Mgr.
Mr. William N. "Bill" Fletcher (1978-1990) Assistant Treasurer and Business Manager
Mr. Harry E. Kellogg (1964-67) Treasurer; 1967-77) Treasurer Emeritus
Rev. Hugo Leinberger (1984-69) Church Planning & Development
Mrs. Opal Moore (1964-66) Office Manager & Bookkeeper
Rev. John B. Muier (1969-78) Camps, Camping and Retreats, Ass't Treasurer and Business Manager
Mr. Russell H. Palmer (1964-67) Assistant Treasurer and Business Manager, Associate for Business Affairs
Mr. George Plews (Interim 1978) Ass't Treas. and Business Mgr.
Rev. C. Theodore Roos (1984-66) Director of Church Life and Work, Director, Church and Society
Rev. J. Robert Sandman (1978-) Conference Minister at Large, Church Planning and Development
Rev. Clara B. Spencer (1985-87) Assoc. Director Christian Education, Church Extension and Planning
Rev. Jeffrey N. Stinehelfer (1983-1990) Director Stewardship and Mission
Rev. Donald G. Stoner (1978-1983) Dir. Stewardship and Interpretation
Dr. Henry N. Tani (1964-65) Dir. Christian Education
Mr. Warren Van Waning (1965-70) Dir. Stewardship and Information
Rev. W. Garver Werntz (Interim 1964-65) Christian Education
Rev. Alfred E. Williams Jr. (1965-78) Minister at Large, Program and Planning, Church and Society, Christian Education, Youth Ministry and Campus Ministry, Division of Parish Life
Mrs. Ethel Windsor (1965) Interim, Dir. Christian Education
Mr. James Parker (1967) Treasurer

CONFERENCE OFFICE SUPPORT STAFF

Mrs. Ethel (Harold C.) Easg (1964-72)
Mrs. Roberta C. (A.M.) Hainer (1961-85)
Mrs. Aldona Kamantas (1984-
Mrs. Lois (Ed. H.) Kay (1982-83)
Mrs. Mary (Walter(Kottemann (1967-
Mrs. Dean (Walter) Kozlak (1971-85)
Mrs. Melinda "Lin" Lexow (1983
Mrs. Charlotte (Richard) Lillquist (1985
Mrs. Mabel Lussow (1960-66)
Mrs. Mary Ellen Randall (1979-84)
Mrs. Evelyn M. Roach (1970-71)
Mrs. Louise (James) Smith (1965-78)
Mrs. Linda S. (Mark) Vanik (1974-
Mrs. Marie (M.L.) Warder (1964-77)
Mrs. Lois S. (Walter) Wenzlaff (1964-74)

ASSOCIATION STAFF

CENTRAL ASSOCIATION:

Associate Conference Ministers

Rev. Louis H. Lammert (1964-68)
Rev. William L. Halfaker (1969-73)
Rev. J. Robert Sandman (1974-79)
Rev. C. Arthur Bradley (1980-

Area Ministers

Rev. Charles D. Hindman (1976-79)
Rev. C. Thomas Jackson (1978-85)
Rev. Karen S. Tyler (Interim, 1986-88)
Rev. Donald S. Beebe (Interim, 1986-87)
Rev. Karen Olm-Stoelting (1988-

CHICAGO METROPOLITAN ASSOCIATION

Associate Conference Ministers

Rev. James R. Smucker (1963-66)
Rev. Frederick Traut (1967-83)
Rev. William Voelkel (1985-

Area Ministers

Rev. Harold B. Dobstaff (1964-74)
Rev. Delbert J. Schrag (1971-89)
Rev. Jimmie L. Sawyer (1980-82)
Rev. Nancy Jo Kemper (Interim, 1983-84)
Rev. Elizabeth Bacon (Interim, 1985)
Rev. Jose Abraham De Jesus (1985-

Northern Association

Associate Conference Ministers

Rev. James D. Stinehelfer (1964-66)
Rev. Edwin J. Hoefer (1967-78)
Rev. Clarence M. Higgins (1978-86)
Rev. Robert C. Meisner (1987-

Area Ministers

Rev. Clarence M. Higgins (1971-78)
Ms. Eleanor Lewis (interim 1978-79)
Rev. Lavon Bayler (1980-

WABASH ASSOCIATION

Pastors-at-Large

Rev. Clare D. Nave (1964)
Rev. Donald R. Scott (1965-68)
Rev. Myrtle Berbout
Rev. William Halfaker (1970-72)
Rev. J. David Thompson (1972-76)
Rev. Carolyn F. Welsh (1976-79)
Rev. Glenn A. Gettinger (1980-84)
Rev. C. Thomas Jackson (1985-87) from Central
Rev. C. Arthur Bradley (1978-89)

ASSOCIATION SUPPORT STAFF

Mrs. Barbara Babcock (Northern)
Mrs. Marion L. (James) Benes (Northern)
Mrs. Ingebord W. Bisanz (Northern)
Mrs. Charlotte Buck (Chicago Metro)
Mrs. Millie (Tom) Clarke (Central)
Mrs. Patricia Davis (Chicago Metro)
Mrs. Pam Espinos (Chicago Metro)
Mrs. Brenda J. Mays (Chicago Metro)
Mrs. Brenda Mitchell (Chicago Metro)
Mrs. Brenda Prather (Northern)
Mrs. Linda Reed (Wabash)
Mrs. Leona (Orville) Schroer (Central)
Mrs. Susan Smith (Central)
Mrs. Sharon Trier (Northern)
Mrs. Paula Tyler (Central)
Mrs. Lois Vahldick (Chicago Metro)
Mrs. Alma (Raymond) Zimmerman (Chicago Metro)

CAMPS

PILGRIM PARK:
- Rev. William D. DeuPree
- Mr. William Bourbon

TOWER HILL:
- Mr. Oliver Rich
- Mr. Herbert A. Martling
- Miss Kathy Stodgell

APPENDIX D: CONFERENCE OFFICERS

MODERATOR:

Co-Moderators:

Rev. M.J.A. Dalrymple,	
Rev. Kurt J. Schmiechen	1964
Mr. William S. Grotfeld	1965
Rev. Joseph C. Cleveland	1966
Mr. Frank H. Mynard	1967
Rev. William S. Mellish	1968
Mr. Elmer L. Beard	1969
Rev. Frederick R. Trost	1970

PRESIDENTS - FROM 1965

Rev. Joseph H. Evans	Rev. Robert D. Schieler
Rev. John L. Schmidt	Mrs. Helen L. Heimburger
Mr. William Gavelek	Rev. Curtis T. Schowalter
Rev. W. Roland Koch	Rev. Harriett N. Martin
Mr. Frank Mynard	Mr. Edward H. Leavitt
Rev. Donald S. Bourne	Rev. Christine D. Barton
Mrs. Arline Barnard	Dr. Manford Byrd Jr.
Rev. James W. Bidle	Rev. Glenn W. Wernecke
Mrs. Robert Cleland	Mrs. Elizabeth Kingsbury
Rev. Wallace W. Reifsteck	Rev. Edward R. Goltz Jr.
Mr. O.C. Gilbert	Mr. George Bell

SECRETARY:

Rev. Dean C. Plassmann	1963-64
Mr. Dawn (R.K.) Wobbe	1964-65
Mrs. Ann (J.P.) Richmond	1966-68

Mrs. Frank C. Green	1969 (called meeting)
Rev. George W. Hirst	1970-72
Mrs. Jane C. (Gilbert) Horn	1973-76
Rev. Sally T. Scheib	1977
Mrs. Helen Heimburger	1978
Rev. Lawrence J. Rezash	1979
Mrs. Julie H. Ullman	1980
Rev. Joel A. Reif	1981-82
Mrs. Patricia Kitner	1983
Rev. Robert C. Ahrendt	1984-87
Ms. Dorothy Auw	1987-

TREASURER:

Mr. Harry E. Kellogg	1965-67
Mrs. James Parker	1967-69
Mr. Gerauld L. Hopkins	1969-71
Mr. Frank H. Mynard Jr.	1972-76
Mr. David W. Overmyer	1977
Mr. Kenneth E. Metcalf	1978-81
Mr. Robert H. White	1982-84
Mrs. Pauline Gallup	1985-87
Rev. Glenn Mensing	1988-

APPENDIX E: ASSOCIATION MODERATORS

CENTRAL:

1965	Rev. Kurt J. Schmiechen
1966	Frank Mynard
1967	Rev. Milo Phillipi
1968	Harry Hyndman Jr.
1969	Rev. Dale Wellbaum
1970	Frank Mynard
1971	Rev. Jonathan B. Story
1972	Ruth (Mrs. Zealy) Holmes
1973	Rev. Walter W. Noffke
1974	William I. Funk
1975	Rev. Wallace W. Reifsteck
1976	Dean Barth
1977	Rev. Ronald C. Christiansen
1978	Helen Heimburger
1979	Rev. Everett E. Seeber
1980	Carl Andres
1981	Rev. Glenn Wernecke
1982	Marion Harding
1983	Rev. Gary Hazlett
1984	Cliff Reynolds
1985	Rev. Arthur R. Koch
1986	George Bell
1987	Rev. Gary Weber
1988	Dorothy (Mrs. Robert) Bizer
1989	Rev. Kenneth Roeder
1990	Ms. Janice Wilson

CHICAGO METROPOLITAN:

1965	Rev. Merl Schiffman
1966	Rev. Glenn Gumm
1967	Mr. Manford Byrd Jr.
1968	Rev. Lionel Miles
1969	Mr. Carl Schoeneberger
1970	Rev. Herbert J. Armstrong
1971	Rev. Edward Bergstraesser
1972	Mrs. Milton Eastman
1973	Rev. Paul Stiffler
1974	Mrs. Robert Cleland
1975	Rev. Lynn McDowell - 1/2 year
1975	Mrs. Robert Cleland - 1/2 year

1976	Mr. Ronald Hanelberg
1977	Rev. Robert Schieler
1978	Mrs. Grace Morris
1979	Rev. Keith Torney
1980	Ms. Susan Thorne
1981	Rev. Eugene Birmingham
1982	Rev. Edward Bergstraesser
1983	Rev. James Duran
1984	Ms. Dorothy Auw
1985	Rev. Alexander Yuille
1986	Mr. Earl Talbot
1987	Rev. Carol Munro Mosley
1988	Ms. Ruth Mojica-Hammer
1989	Rev. Robert Ridenour
1990	Ms. Dorothy Dill

NORTHERN:

1964-65	Rev. Walter W. Bloesch
1965-66	Ms. Edna Speer
1966-67	Rev. William S. Mellish
1967-68	Glen E. True
1968-69	Rev. Stanley Schmidt
1969-70	J.G. Hadcock
1970-71	Rev. Curtis T. Schowalter
1971-72	Ms. Frances Wheeler
1972-73	Rev. Grafton M. Thomas
1973-74	Ms. Alice Bryant
1974-75	Rev. Arthur W. Christofersen
1975-76	Mr. William Gavelek
1976-77	Rev. George W. Hohmann
1977-78	Ms. Barbara Ballard
1978-79	Rev. Philip J. Anstedt
1979-80	Mr. Paul Muenchow
1980-81	Rev. Glenn F. Mensing
1981-82	Mr. Eugene Hellwer
1982-83	Rev. W. Melvin Hough
1983-84	Ms. Jean Plews
1984-85	Rev. Richard E. Nye
1985-86	Ms. Patricia Anderson
1986-87	Rev. William Nagy
1987-88	Ms. Patricia Anderson
1988-89	Rev. Warren Mueller
1989-90	Ms. Thelma Thornton
1990-91	Rev. Gladys Herzog

WABASH:

1963-72	Rev. Carl D. Hall
1972-78	Mrs. Mary Lee Beckes
1979-81	Mrs. Conrades Christy
1982-85	Earl Brooks
1985-89	Rev. David Reed
1989	Rev. Steve Batman

CONFERENCE COUNCIL (Dates of first term)

Acosta, Rev. Samuel	1975
Aguilar, Mrs. Esther	1987
Aguilar, Rev. Nicanor	1989
Akemann, Rev. Peter	1985
Allen, Samuel	1977
Alward, Rev. Robert S.	1979
Anderson, Mrs. Pat	1987
Andrews, James T.	1983
Anstedt, Rev. Philip	1978
Auw, Ms. Dorothy	1983
Bachman, Mrs. Alice	1974
Bayler, Rev. Lavon A.	1974
Beardon, Rev. Newton	1984
Bizer, Mrs. Dorothy	1987
Beckes, Mrs. Mary Lee	1975
Bender, Michael J.	1974
Bergstraesser, Rev. Edward W.	1982
Bermann, William E.	1976
Bernard, Mrs. Edmund	1972
Bobsin, William Jr.	1984
Blumberg, Rev. Robert J.	1983
Bourne, Rev. Donald S.	1968
Bradshaw, Mrs. Marvin	1964
Brooks, Earl L.	1982
Bryant, Mrs. Alice	1973
Burton, Rev. George E.	1978
Cantrell, Rev. James H.	1979
Carson, Mrs. Gordon	1969
Christiansen, Rev. Donald C.	
Christofersen, Rev. Arthur W.	1974
Christopher, Rev. James A.	1984
Christy, Rev. Carey	1969
Christy, Mrs. Conrades	1976
Clay, Rev. Joseph P.	1969
Cordes, Emerson	1984
Cordts, Mrs. Ralph	1969
Correll, Leo	1964
Cronenberg, Mrs. Ruby	1988
Cump, Percy	1968
Chevrier, Rev. David	1973
Chapman, Rev. Gary	1983
Davis, Rev. Herbert R.	1966
Eades, Donald	1974
Eastman, Mrs. Milton	1971
Edmunds, Arthur W.	1964
Eggers, Herbert	1974
Eggleston, Edward	1977
Eickelmann, Mrs. Mary Ann	1979
Elkins, Mrs. Robert	1972
Ellersieck, Rev. Arthur P.	1972
Elliott, Rev. James H.	1976
Ellis, Rev. Thomas H.	1971
Engestrom, Filke	1969
Erwin, Rev. Clyde V.	1966
Evans, Rev. Randall H.	1973
Ewing, Mrs. Sharon	1984
Fasules, Mrs. Lenore	1969
Fraccaro, Rev. Joseph	1980
Gavelek, William	1966
German, Fred	1964
Goltz, Rev. Edward B.	1987
Gonzales, Rev. James	1980
Goodwin, James	1968
Grandgeorge, Mrs. Genevieve	1968
Green, Mrs. Frank C.	1968
Griesenaue, Theodore	1964

Griffin, Rev. Arthur D.	1988
Gumm, Rev. Glenn C.	1967
Hall, Rev. Carl D.	1966
Hamelberg, Ronald	1976
Harding, Rev. Edward L.	1975
Harper, Rev. L. Alexander	1986
Hartz, Rev. George F.	1974
Hatfield, Rev. Robert E. Jr.	1986
Hazlett, Rev. Gary R.	1982
Heimburger, Mrs. Helen	1977
Heller, Eugene B.	1982
Herro, Mrs. Jean	1977
Hohmann, Rev. George W.	1976
Hobart, James	1970
Hoglund, Dr. William C.	1968
Holmes, Mrs. Zealy	1971
Horn, Mrs. Gilbert	1964
Hough, Rev. W. Melvin	1983
Hunyady, Rev. Laslo O.	1971
Hyndman, Harry L.	1978
Jacobs, Rev. Robert F.	1979
Johnson, Mrs. Clarence	1964
Johnson, Mrs. Harry H.	1966
Johnson, Rev. Lanning L.	1974
Jackson, Rev. Robert Q.	1988
Kasper, Rev. Robert E.	1972
Keller, Mrs. Dorothy	1974
Kellogg, Henry	1966
Kidd, Rev. James L.	1976
Kingsbury, Mrs. Petty	1980
Kleffmann, Rev. Walter H.	1964
Klueter, Rev. John H.	1971
Kniker, Rev. David F.	1973
Koch, Rev. Arthur W.	1982
Koch, Rev. W. Rowland	1964
Kuhfuss, William	1980
Kutz, Mrs. Gerald	1971
Lambrecht, Mrs. Paul	1966
Leavitt, Edward H.	1984
Lewis, Dorothy	1973
Libert, Rev. John H.	1982
Luckey, Mrs. Linda L.	1988
Mahar, Mrs. Frank	1966
Mayer, Rev. Charles F.	1983
Mardis, Rev. Herbert H.	1967
Martin, Rev. Harriet N.	1982
McConnell, Mrs. Donald	1964
McDowell, Rev. Lynn	1975
Mealiff, Mrs. Ernest	1969
Means, Mrs. J.	1973
Mellish, Rev. Stanley	1969
Mensing, Rev. Glenn F.	1971
Metcalf, Kenneth E.	1978
Miles, Rev. Lionel A.	1964
Miller, Rev. Clyde H. Jr.	1967
Morris, Mrs. Frace	
Moulthrop, Rev. George A.	1985
Mueller, Rev. Warren J.	1984
Mueller, Rev. Warren M.	1978
Muenchow, Paul	1979
Mulvihill, Edward P.	1969
Munro, Rev. Carol	1987
Myers, Kenneth	1966
Mynard, Frank H.	1966
Mynard, Frank H. III	1976
Nave, Rev. Clare	1964
Nelson, Ms. Nancy	1986
Nye, Rev. Richard E.	1984
Palmer, Mrs. Janet	1980
Parker, James	1968
Ping, Mrs. Phoebe	1985
Plassmann, Rev. Dean G.	1964
Press, Rev. Kenneth R.	1967
Price, Mrs. Arthur	1964
Queen, Rev. John S.	1966
Rabenstein, Mrs. Francis	1986
Reed, Rev. David D.	1986
Reif, Rev. Joel A.	1982
Reifsteck, Rev. Wallace W.	1966
Reynolds, Cliff	1983
Rezash, Rev. Lawrence J.	1973
Richmond, Mrs. J.P.	1966
Rohr, Mrs. Elsworth	1974
Roser, Mrs. Elizabeth	1977
Roser, Foster	1976
Roeder, Rev. Kenneth F.	1988
Rust, Rev. Henry	1975
Schaper, Rev. Arnold D.	1967

Scheuer, Rev. Garry A.	1973
Schieler, Rev. Robert D.	1977
Schmidt, Rev. John L.	1964
Schmidt, Russell	1981
Schmiechen, Rev. Kurt	1964
Schmuddle, Al	1985
Schowalter, Rev. Curtis T.	1970
Schrag, Rev. Delbert J.	1970
Schriefer, Mrs. Lorraine	1979
Seeber, Rev. Everett E.	1978
Seyfert, Rev. Warren H.	1967
Smith, Rev. Lester E.	1967
Smith, Mrs. Louise	1982
Stratemeyer, Rev. Arthur R.	1981
Swain, Theodore W.	1972
Swanson, Mrs. Hayes	1968
Sherry, Rev. Paul H.	1985
Talbot, Earl A.	1986
Tape, Ms. Marian E.	1986
Thompkins, Rev. Eddie C.	1981
Thorne, Rev. Susan	1981
Torney, Rev. E. Keith	1971
Traut, Rev. Fred G.	1967
Triebel, Rev. Thomas F.	1988
Trost, Rev. Frederick E.	1975
True, Glen E.	1963
Tupper, Gerald R.	1977
Vahldick, Mrs. Lois	1980
Veatch, Roger	1977
Van Lackum, Rev. Nancy Jo	1981
Ward, Mrs. John M.	1971
Warkentin, Rev. Jacob M.	1964
Webber, Mrs. Rosa	1974
Weir, Dr. Edgar	1964
Wellbaum, Rev. Dale R.	1964
Webber, Rev. Gary R.	1986
West, Rev. Richard	1975
Wernecke, Rev. Glenn W.	1981
Wheeler, Mrs. Edward K.	1964
White, Robert B.	1980
Whiten, Rev. Bennie	1984
Whitener, Ray	1970
Wildman, Rev. Charles L.	1976
Williamson, Jeff.	1983
Wiltberger, Richard	1964
Woodruff, Mrs. Joseph A.	1966
Zillgitt, Rev. Arthur D.	1989
Zinn, Rev. J. Robert	1985
Zinn, Laini	1988